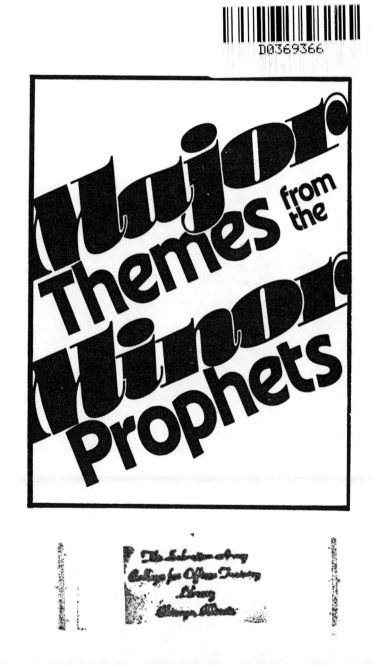

Major **Themes** from the Minor **Prophets**

Gerald H. Twombly

BMH Books
Winona Lake, Indiana 46590

To my Mother,
Minita Twombly,
and my Grandmother,
Myrtle Cooley
in fond appreciation
of my godly heritage
(2 Timothy 1:5)

Cover design by Timothy Kennedy

ISBN: 0-88469-132-2

Printed in U.S.A.

Preface

The challenge of producing a volume on the Minor Prophets was one that I accepted with enthusiasm. I have long considered these short twelve books to be some of the most up-to date in the Bible. While the circumstances have changed over the centuries, the relevance of these penetrating messages to contemporary society has never been more needed than today. The discerning descriptions to be found of nations and people will prick the hardest of hearts. You may wonder that if only "the names were changed," God might be pronouncing through these prophets His wrath on those today who willfully spurn His revelation. Certainly the character of God has never changed, and that fact alone justifies our careful attention to His acts of the past.

I am grateful for the assistance provided by so many in the production of this volume. It was in the serene setting of Timber Point Farm on the tranquil shores of the Atlantic Ocean where most of this work found its final form. My family is to be thanked for their encouragement and willingness to let me "hide away" many of the mornings of our annual vacation retreat. I wish to express thanks to my devoted friend and colleague, Dr. Charles Smith, for the resource materials he made available to enhance my research. Dr. John Whitcomb's willingness to allow the reproduction of his valuable chart "Old Testament Kings and Prophets" is most appreciated.

As you read these pages, it is my prayer that they will broaden your scriptural understanding and challenge you to commit your life anew to our blessed Saviour.

—Gerald H. Twombly

Winona Lake, Indiana

Table of Contents

Preface 5

Introduction 9

Old Testament Kings and Prophets Chart 16

1. Hosea: The Price of Unfaithfulness 17

2. Joel: Jehovah's Army 29

3. Amos: Israel Out of Plumb 39

4. Obadiah: The Fall of Edom 49

5. Jonah: The Prophet Who Ran Away 57

6. Micah: The King Is Coming 71

7. Nahum: Reaping the Whirlwind 85

8. Habakkuk: The Just Shall Live by Faith 95

9. Zephaniah: Prophet of Royal Blood 105

10. Haggai: The Prophet that Motivated 113

11. Zechariah: God's Message from the Myrtle Grove . . 121

12. Malachi: Prophet to the Indifferent 133

Introduction

Frequently when preaching from the Old Testament prophets, I encourage people to turn to that section of their Bible where the pages still stick together. The statement generally brings smiles among the congregation as everyone flips to a portion of the Bible too often ignored. Inevitably that portion to which they turn are the books we are about to study; those we designate as the Minor Prophets.

The Minor Prophets were so named because their writings were so much smaller in bulk than the prophecies of Isaiah, Jeremiah, and Ezekiel. In the Hebrew Bible they were bound together as one, after a rabbinical tradition quoted by Kimchi, "lest one or other of them should be lost on account of its size, if they were all kept separate."

The prophets lived at a critical period of history and their messages were uttered as the "Word of God" to a generation who needed to hear. Keil declares that, when taken "with the writings of the greater prophets, they comprehend all the essentials of that prophetic word, through which the Lord equipped His people for the coming times of conflict with the nations of the world, endowing them thus with the light and power of His Spirit, and causing His servants to foretell, as a warning to the ungodly, the destruction of the two sinful kingdoms, and the dispersion of the rebellious people among the heathen and, as a consolation to believers, the deliverance and preservation of a holy seed, and the eventual triumph of His kingdom over every hostile power." The prophet was cognizant that His word was from God as the phrase "thus saith the Lord" prefaced his message more than 1,200 times!

Message of the Old Testament Prophets

G. F. Oehler took the view that the messages of the prophets were committed to writing that, "when fulfilled, they might prove to future generations the righteousness and faithfulness of the covenant of God, and that they might serve until then as a lamp to the righteous, enabling them, even in the midst of the darkness of the coming times of judgment, to understand the ways of God in His kingdom." Certainly the prophets occupy a unique role in the providential development of history as they boldly declare the whole counsel of God. Five features of the prophetic message deserve special attention:

The times of the prophets. The prophets were sent in times of apostasy and rebellion. Their primary message was one of protest against present conditions and of calling men back to God. This was the "forth-telling" aspect of their ministry.

The nature of their message. The message of the prophets sometimes had a double fulfillment. In many cases only part of what the prophet said was fulfilled in his time with complete fulfillment reserved until a later time. This represents the "fore-telling" aspect of their message.

The source of their message. The message that the prophets spoke was a product of direct and special revelation from God. There was an undeniable quality about what they said and despite the resistance of men they boldly rested on the authority and authenticity of their revelation.

The focus of the prophetic message. The focus of Old Testament prophecy is upon the two advents of Christ.

The exclusions of Old Testament prophecy. Two significant omissions occur in the message of the Old Testament prophets. There is no reference to the church which Paul later reveals to be "the mystery" of God, and Gentiles are mentioned only in relationship to their dealings with Israel.

Three Important Facts

There are three very elementary but significant facts that every student of the Old Testament prophets must grasp if he is to gain an adequate understanding of this portion of God's revelation.

The first of these has to do with the division of the nation of Israel after the death of Solomon. The event is recorded in 1 Kings 12 and represents the single most significant event to affect the understanding of the prophets in the Bible. Upon Solomon's death the northern areas of his dominion seceded and gained independence under their own king, Jeroboam. The southern area became known as Judah and clung to its Davidic heritage. The first Judean king was Rehoboam. From this point on in Old Testament history (the time of the division was approximately 930 B.C.), revelation from God when directed to His people was addressed to either the nation of Israel or Judah.

A second fact that needs to be comprehended thoroughly by the student of the Old Testament, is that the revelation we possess *is not* in chronological order. In fact, historical progression ends with the Old Testament Book of Esther (with the exception of Malachi who wrote after the events recorded in Esther). The poetical and prophetical books that conclude the order of the Old Testament are actually supplemental to the material included in the books of history (especially Samuel through Kings).

The third issue needed to be understood has to do with the captivities. The prophets frequently announced a time of judgment when the nations of Israel and Judah would suffer at the hands of foreign invaders. In the case of the Israelites, the nation Assyria was the providential tool of God in issuing His righteous judgment. The armies of Assyria eventually destroyed Israel's capital after a long siege in 722 B.C. and deported many of the surviving remnant. It was not until over 135 years later that King Nebuchadnezzar led the armies of Babylon against Jerusalem. In 586 B.C. the glorious capital of Judah was in ruins and a mangled remnant torn away to live in Babylon. Prophets to Israel recognize the Assyrian threat and preach repentance in lieu of military destruction. Judah's prophets foresee the onslaught of the Babylonians. It is a comprehension of these events and an accompanying understanding of the strategic balance of power struggle that will make the prophets live as you read their informative pages.

The Designation of the Prophets

Several students of the Old Testament have suggested means to designate these writings we call the prophets. Their categorizations satisfy our need for organization and enable us to better grasp a great bulk of God's revelation to us.

The most frequent and familiar of these divisions is that alluded to by the title of this book. It distinguishes between those longer books of the prophets (Isaiah, Jeremiah-Lamentations, Ezekiel— the "Major Prophets") with those smaller in size (Hosea, Joel, Amos, Obadiah, Jonah, Micah, Nahum, Habakkuk, Zephaniah, Haggai, Zechariah, Malachi—the "Minor Prophets").

Others have chosen to divide the prophetic books around the periods of exile. There are those that are prior to the captivity of Israel (Pre-Exilic to Israel)—Jonah, Amos and Hosea; those that were written prior to the captivity of Judah (Pre-Exilic to Judah)—Obadiah, Joel, Isaiah, Micah, Nahum, Habakkuk, Zephaniah and Jeremiah; those that were written during the exile (Exilic)—Ezekiel and Daniel (although Daniel is technically not one of the prophets); and those that were written after the exile (Post-Exilic writings were to Judah only)—Haggai, Zechariah and Malachi.

Still others have divided the books around the time period in which they were written. Six were written around the time of Assyria's domination (Joel, Jonah, Amos, Hosea, Isaiah and Micah); seven were written during Babylon's dominant influence in the middle east (Jeremiah, Ezekiel, Daniel, Obadiah, Nahum, Habakkuk and Zephaniah), and three wrote around the time of the restoration (Haggai, Zechariah and Malachi).

Another designation centers around the recipients to the prophetic messages. Amos and Hosea address their messages predominantly to Israel; Jonah and Nahum have a special message to Nineveh; Odabiah prophecies the destruction of Edom; while the others (Joel, Isaiah, Micah, Jeremiah, Habakkuk, Zephaniah, Ezekiel, Haggai, Zechariah, and Malachi) minister specifically to the nation Judah.

Diagnosing the Hardened Heart

True religion is more than a profession. It is a manner of life, the roots of which are grounded deep in the revelation of God. Zechariah was commanded of the Lord to remind Judah that God's will for them was to"Dispense true justice and practice kindness and compassion each to his brother, and do not oppress the widow or the orphan, the stranger or the poor; and do not devise evil in your hearts against one another" (Zech. 7:9-10). The brother of our Lord wrote similar words: "This is pure and undefiled religion in the sight of our God and Father, to visit orphans and widows in their distress, and to keep oneself unstained by the world" (James 1:27).

The practice of righteousness was something that was seldom seen during the ministries of the prophets. People's hearts had become hardened and the Word of the Lord failed to even penetrate their self-deafened ears.

Zechariah describes the observable process in which a heart "becomes like flint" in chapter 11 and verses 11 and 12. Perhaps four revealing questions might be asked to diagnose the condition of the human heart, while adequately summarizing this discerning message. Carefully consider the following:

Can you neglect a known and observable need? When Zechariah reflected on life prior to the captivity he noted that the nation as a whole "refused to pay attention" (Zech. 7:11) to their known responsibilities. They could see a need and willfully turn their back to it. This indifference would lead to their judgment.

Is the Church of Jesus Christ indifferent to the needs of those around us in our day? Can we as individuals walk passed others with need and then rationalize our insensitivity by saying, "Not today," or "I just don't have time," or "I can't get involved"? The first step to a hardened heart is indifference.

Do you continually reject known responsibilities without conviction? The prophet went on to observe that the nation had "turned a stubborn shoulder." Indifference to someone's need is one thing, but a refusal to ignore that which we know is right is stubbornness.

Stubbornness is an acquired trait. A person is not born stubborn, but only becomes that way when allowed to persist. The nation Judah had come to a point in their history where their own self interests and concerns took priority over the will of God. This reckless attitude was observable in their relationship with others.

Do you gratefully receive biblical admonition? Zechariah wrote, "and they stopped their ears from hearing" (Zech. 7:11). They willfully "turned off" God and the message of His prophets in favor of pursuing their own interests.

How do we receive rebuke? When hearing a message from God that pricks our hearts, do we express our appreciation and thanks or do we become even more committed to the pursuit of our desires? Not only has that one with a hardened heart rejected known responsibilities, he has rejected the convicting counsel of God.

Do you hear at all? We are told that the nation had willfully made their hearts like flint (Zech. 7:12). There came a point where their sinful pursuits had taken total control and no longer were they even capable of hearing God's truth. The process was complete.

It was to men with "hardened hearts" that God sent His prophets. In the majority of cases their divine message rolled off backs like water off the proverbial duck. As we approach the study of these books, might it be that we have allowed our hearts to become hardened? God's message to His people was to repent. God's message to those in a similar state is the same!

A Relevant Message

Perhaps the greatest excuse given by modern man for ignoring the prophetic writings is that they hold no relevance to contemporary society. It should be noted that the prophets were men who spoke to their own time; they had a message from God to their own generation and nation. But while their message had a particular pertinence to that period, there is a special significance for our time. God's character is changeless and no better purpose can be served than to devote our time to the study of His ways.

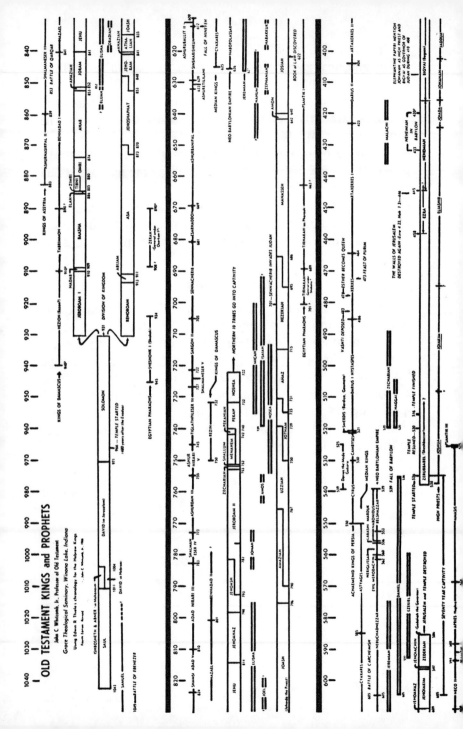

OLD TESTAMENT KINGS and PROPHETS

John C. Whitcomb, Jr., Professor of Old Testament

Grace Theological Seminary, Winona Lake, Indiana

Using Edwin R. Thiele's chronology for the Hebrew Kings

Fourth Edition Revised   John C. Whitcomb Jr. 1986

1

Hosea: The Price of Unfaithfulness

KEYS THAT UNLOCK HOSEA

I.   The Time of the Book: Hosea was a Pre-Exilic Prophet who wrote to the nation of Israel.

II. The Contemporaries of the Prophet: The prophets Amos, Jonah, Isaiah, and possibly Micah ministered at the same time as the prophet Hosea.

III. The Theme of the Book: The theme of the Book of Hosea is "Unfaithfulness Condemned."

IV. The Key Verse of the Book: "You have plowed wickedness, you have reaped injustice, you have eaten the fruit of lies, because you have trusted in your way . . ." (Hosea 10:13).

V.   Background Reading: A good preparation to the study of Hosea would be to read 2 Kings 14–20 and 2 Chronicles 26–32.

Introducing his study of the Book of Hosea, J. Sidlow Baxter refers to Hosea as "the prophet of Israel's zero hour." The point so clearly made is that the nation had sunk so low and had become so corrupt that nothing could be done to avert God's righteous judgment.

In order to understand the message of this significant book, it is imperative that one grasp a feeling for the times of this most unusual prophet. Called to the prophetic ministry during the reign of Jeroboam II of Israel (1:1), Hosea was a contemporary of Amos and Isaiah. He lived in a period of material and political prosperity. Life seemed secure; but, despite this appearance of tranquillity, the stage was already being set for an outpouring of divine wrath not before seen by the nation of Israel. The measure of a nation's blessing rests not in its prosperity but in the souls of its people, and it was here that Israel had sunk to deplorable depths. Pusey refers to this in his book *The Minor Prophets* saying:

> Every commandment of God was broken, and that habitually. All was falsehood, adultery, bloodshedding; deceit to God produced faithlessness to man; excess and luxury were supplied by secret or open robbery, oppression, false dealing, perversion of justice, grinding of the poor. Blood was shed like water.... Adultery was consecrated as an act of religion. Those who were first in rank were first in excess. People and king vied in debauchery, and the sottish king joined and encouraged the freethinkers and blasphemers of his court. The idolatrous priests loved and shared in the sins of the people; nay, they seem to have set themselves to intercept those on either side of Jordan, who would go to worship at Jerusalem, laying wait to murder them. Corruption had spread throughout the whole land.... Remonstrance was useless, the knowledge of God was willfully rejected; the people hated rebuke.

This description depicted life *characteristic* among the people at the time of Hosea's ministry. More unfortunate is the fact that people seemed all but unaware of their need for spiritual revival.

Amos and Hosea

The similarities and differences between this prophecy of Hosea and that of his bold contemporary, Amos, are dealt with by Everett Harrison in his *Introduction to the Old Testament*. He writes:

> Whereas his contemporary Amos denounced social inequalities and the exploitation of the lower classes, Hosea was concerned primarily with moral, religious and political abominations in the nation.... For Amos iniquity consisted in the failure of Israel to meet the divine demand for righteousness. For Hosea, sinfulness was envisaged in terms of the breaking of a covenant or agreement that needed by definition to be honored by both the participants.

Hosea is depicted by one writer to be the "prophet of outraged but persevering love"; while Amos is seen as a prophet of the law. Despite these differences, they both bore a divine message condemning the people for their sinful behavior and announcing the certainty of divine judgment.

Style and Outline

Tatford refers to Hosea's style as "patently the product of the educated class." The prophet uses metaphors and similes and resorts to multiplied illustrations to reinforce the impact of his words. There is frequent use of puns (sometimes lost in the English translation). The unhappy marital experience of the prophet clearly affected the character of his preaching and served as a vivid picture of the spiritual infidelity of the nation.

The opening three chapters of the book tell the story of Hosea's tragic marriage and serve as a prologue to the entire prophetic message. Utilizing the outline of Baxter in his extraordinary *Explore the Book* the remaining chapters might be divided as follows: Israel's Sin Is Intolerable: God Is Holy (4-7), Israel Shall Be Punished: God Is Just (8-10) and Israel Shall Be Restored: God Is Love (11-14). It will be around these major divisions that we shall restrict our comments.

The Prologue

The opening three chapters of the prophecy tell the symbolic story of Hosea's unfaithful wife and her children. Before Hosea commenced his prophetic ministry, he was instructed of the Lord to acquire a wife. The command was a strange one, "Go and take yourself a wife of harlotry and children of harlotry" (1:2).

Because of the moral difficulties inherent in the marriage of a prophet of God and a prostitute, a number of views have commanded the attention of commentators. The issue predominantly debated has to do with whether or not Gomer (Hosea's wife) was given to immorality at the time of the marriage. The issue is accentuated, at least in the minds of many, by the implication of the text that her infidelity was known to the prophet at the time of the union.

The marriage was obviously intended to be symbolic of Israel's union with Jehovah. In keeping with that symbolism, it would seem logical that the immorality of Gomer occurred *after* the marital union. The Israel whom God originally espoused was innocent (Jer. 2:2) and devoted to Him. It was only later that the seductions of the gods of Caanan prompted spiritual infidelity. This was the position of C. I. Scofield who wrote: "God did not command Hosea to take an immoral wife but permitted him to carry out his desire to marry Gomer, warning him that she would be unfaithful, and using the prophet's sad experience as a basis for the presentation of lessons about God's relation to Israel." Many others concur on concluding that Hosea had no idea of Gomer's inclinations and it was only long after the fateful marriage that God directed Hosea to write the words which introduce his message. Whether or not one takes this position or adopts the view that Hosea, willingly and knowingly, took an immoral wife, it should be made clear that God in neither case asked Hosea to sin.

The message of Hosea became, as one writer puts it, "the essential catalyst for the mediation of God's Word." It was the heartbreak of his own marriage that caused Hosea to see Israel's sin against God in its deepest and most real significance.

Gomer bore three children whose names are provided in the text. Like the actual marital union, each child symbolically bore a special message to the nation Israel. The significance of each name deserves special consideration:

Jezreel ("God Sows"). Hosea was commanded of the Lord to name the firstborn son "Jezreel" (1:3). The name brought immediate recognition. The valley of Jezreel, a fertile plain between the mountains of Galilee and Samaria, had been the site of many fierce battles. It was at the town of Jezreel, at the southern edge of the valley, that Jehu slew Jehoram and Jezebel of Israel and Ahaziah of Judah (2 Kings 9:24–10:11). Although primarily in fulfillment of the divine commission, Jehu's deceitful and bloody deeds went far beyond the commission given him by the prophet Elisha (2 Kings 9:7).

The birth of Jezreel proclaimed that God would avenge the "blood of Jezreel" and that one day God would "break the bow of Israel" in this valley known elsewhere in Scripture as Esdraelon or Armageddon (see Zech. 14:1, Rev. 16:16).

Lo-ruhamah ("Without Pity or Compassion"). The second child born to Gomer was apparently illegitimate. The Lord instructed the prophet to name the daughter Lo-ruhamah, meaning "without pity or compassion."

The message to the nation is made clear by the revelation Hosea received from the Lord. Because of their gross neglect of God and their spiritual idolatry, God would no longer show compassion upon the nation of Israel. Judah, for the time being, would be delivered by God; not because of their military preparedness, but because of their faithfulness to Him. Frederick Tatford refers to the announcement concerning the nation Judah (Hosea 1:7) in his book *Prophet of a Broken Home*, saying: "The reference is almost undoubtedly to the miraculous deliverance of Jerusalem in 701 B.C. The army of Sennacherib invaded Judah, but as Isaiah promised, the Assyrian host was routed—not as the result of battle nor by the military might of Hezekiah, but by the hand of God. The angel of Jehovah slew 185,000 Assyrians in the night (2 Kings 19:35)."

Lo-ammi ("Not My People"). The third child born to Gomer appears, too, to have been born out of an adulterous relationship. The daughter was named Lo-ammi, meaning, "not my people." The lesson to Israel was that their sin had separated them from God and He would have no part in their wicked ways. This was the very antithesis of promises made to the nation Israel in the past (see Exod. 6:7, Deut. 26:17-18) and reveals the awful extent of their sin and the breach between God and the nation that it created.

The opening chapter ends with a remarkable promise that one day God would again embrace His people (1:10-11). The promise is a reminder that God's covenant with Abraham was unconditional and irrevocable and nothing could annul it (Gal. 3:17). Israel's sin would be judged, but God would eventually fulfill His promises to the nation.

As one concludes his study of the opening chapters, he should remember that these initial three chapters provide a prologue to the prophetic message of Hosea. The second and third chapters amplify the response of the prophet to his situation and symbolically picture the attitude that God would take to a wayward Israel.

Israel's Sin Is Intolerable

The intolerable sin of Israel is described in the next section of Hosea's prophecy (Hosea, chapters 4 through 7). It was sin that violated divine holiness and separated a people from their God. In my book *An Analytical Survey of the Bible,* I have noted five specific charges against Israel that provided a basis for the judgment that was imminent. A review of these five points will provide a review of these significant chapters.

Israel would be judged for a lack of knowledge (4:6). Knowledge is the foundation of spiritual understanding. Not only had Israel failed in appropriating the provisions of God, but they also had stubbornly resisted acquiring the knowledge that was essential if they were to live godly lives. The resultant sin was inevitable. Apart from a knowledge of God, acquired through His authoritative revelation, men lack the wherewithal to overcome the subtle attacks of Satan.

The priesthood was particularly guilty of dispensing knowledge to the people and had failed miserably. R. F. Horton writes concerning these priests that they had "turned religion into ritual, and had neglected the instruction in the knowledge of God . . . their two primary functions."

Israel would be judged for lack of growth (4:16). Apart from the infusion of the soul with the "knowledge of God" there can be no spiritual growth. The chosen of God are referred to by the prophet as "a backsliding heifer" (4:16), pathetically unable to progress. An entire nation had lost its spiritual sensitivity and walked aimlessly in a corrupt world. Efforts for reform were weakly rooted in the ground of selfishness and for every step attempted forward the nation was sliding back two.

It has been suggested that the nation had come to the point of no return. So imprisoned by the grip of their evil deeds, the nation was unable to free itself. R. L. Honeycutt says in his commentary that "a man's deeds or actions become the obsessive, compulsive power of his life. They prevent him from making that quality of reflective appraisal which will lead to return and renewal. Sin robs man of his faculty for God and strength of will to obey God." It was the lack of knowledge that caused them to sin and it was sin that bound them helplessly for judgment!

Israel would be judged for lack of separation (4:17; 7:4, 8). Syncretism was so complete that there was no discernable difference between Israel and the people of the land. The nation Israel had adopted the idol worship characteristic of the heathen and had sunk to such depths that Hosea proclaimed, "they are all adulterors" (7:4).

Satan offers to the world religion without God, an appealing offer to some but a meaningless exercise in futility. Israel had compromised away her day of opportunity and had lost her identity in the process. Walking the fence of spiritual mediocrity resulted in national disaster!

Israel would be judged for a lack of humility (5:5, 13:6). Perhaps the greatest enemy to true revival is the pride of men. It is condemnatory. The pride of Israel would testify against her in the court of heaven. Writes Tatford, "It was legal terminology: God Himself would give evidence in His own court, which would condemn the guilty nation. They were without defense and would stumble when the sentence was pronounced."

Israel would be judged for a lack of prayer (7:14). Because of their sin, God withheld from the nation the produce of the soil (see 4:3, 9:2). In the midst of the accompanying turmoil, the nation "wailed upon their beds" (7:14) rather than seeking forgiveness and the blessing of God. They regarded Jehovah as little more than an alternative to the gods of the land. One has written that "they merely treated Him as the equivalent of Baal. What they would have done in the Canaanite ritual, they actually performed. They cut themselves as did the followers of Baal (1 Kings 18:28), as though this self-mutilation would appeal to Jehovah. This action was forbidden by the law (Deut. 14:1), although it was habitually practiced in the country." These attitudes were intolerable to God and would result in the outpouring of His wrath.

Several analogies are used by Hosea to depict the awful character of the sin of the nation. The prophet declared that they were as an adulterous wife (3:1), a backsliding heifer (4:11), a drunkard (4:11), troops of robbers (6:9), hot as an oven (7:7), a half-baked cake (7:8), a silly dove (7:11), a crooked bow (7:16), a broken vessel (8:8), and a wild ass (8:9).

Israel Shall Be Punished

Chapters 8 through 10 of Hosea's prophecy speak of the judgment that God was about to inflict upon the nation of Israel. The key verse of this book is found in this section. It is

Hosea 10:13: "You have plowed wickedness, you have reaped injustice, you have eaten the fruit of lies, because you have trusted in your way . . . ." The physical law that "every action is responded to with an equal and opposite reaction" has its parallel in the realm of the spiritual (see Gal. 6:7). The divine indignation over Israel's sin reaches its pinnacle as Hosea announces that the nation was about to reap the consequences of her continual sin. Three progressive steps of that judgment are alluded to by the prophet:

The nation would find no satisfaction in their religious activity (8:13, 9:4). It seems strangely paradoxical that a nation so devoted to sin would be religiously active. As Hosea and his contemporary Amos ministered in Israel's cities they would have seen a number of sacrificial altars. While many of these altars were constructed to the foreign gods of Canaan, there were "Jehovah Worshippers" who sought to appease God by the proliferation of animal sacrifices. Their sacrifices were unavailing: they were the gifts of insincere men, and God rejected them.

Words of a former prophet to Israel's King Saul staggered the self-righteous monarch. In the king's efforts to rationalize away his disobedience, he claimed to have spared and sacrificed animals "in thanksgiving" to God for the victory he had achieved. When Samuel heard the king's feeble excuse for his sinful act, he responded that obedience is better than sacrifice (see 1 Sam. 15:22). The sin of this later date received a similar response by God! Religious activity is meaningless apart from a contrite heart.

The produce of the field was divinely withheld (8:7). On more than one occasion God exercised His sovereign authority over nature to try His people. The prophecy of Joel tells of an incredible locust plague that was ordained of God to bring men to repentance. Hosea speaks of Israel's lack of agricultural productivity as God's means of condemning the nation for its evil conduct.

Israel would be taken captive by the Assyrians (8:9). Hosea announced that Israel would become absorbed by the nations. The means that the nation used to protect themselves against foreign aggression, primarily the negotiation of alliances with allies, worked to the detriment of Israel who was losing her unique identity through compromise. Assyria would invade Israel and eventually destroy the nation, taking captive the surviving remnant.

Israel *would* "reap the whirlwind" because of her unrighteousness. Israel had failed to respond to the intermediate steps of God to bring her to repentance. The nation eventually lost all spiritual sensitivity and could not even recognize a word from God through His prophet. There was no alternative to judgment; it was inevitable.

Israel Shall Be Restored

The final chapters of Hosea reaffirm the necessity and inevitability of judgment (11:5-6, 13:3, 7-8, 13). There is a noticeable change in tone (especially observable in chapter 11), however, referred to by Moulton as "the yearning of God." The eleventh chapter alludes to God's remarkable love for Israel (see vv. 4, 8-9, 10-11) which with sorrow regrets the necessity of the punitive action about to take place.

The final chapter provides the orchestrated climax of that great love that God has for Israel. This is the final triumph of love when, as Baxter writes, "judgment is finished, sin is forgiven, backsliding is healed and love reigns." Israel will again be restored, her long plunder will have accomplished its purpose and Israel will once more exhibit its exalted position among the nations of the world.

The prophecy of Hosea not only deals with the working of God with Israel, but it also sets out divine principles through which God deals with mankind. The prophet appropriately concludes his message with a call to men to understand God's ways (14:9). Tatford writes, "The ways of Jehovah become paths to be trodden by the enlightened. They are right or straight paths which lead undeviatingly to the right end. The upright wisely walk in such ways, appreciating that they lead unerringly to the heart of God." Transgressors only stumble because they have failed to comprehend the heart and mind of God. It is the Word of God that magnifies His ways, "Thy word is a lamp to my feet, and a light to my path" (Ps. 119:105).

How well do we understand God's ways?

2

Joel: Jehovah's Army

KEYS THAT UNLOCK JOEL

I. The Time of the Book: Joel is a pre-exilic prophet to Judah. He is probably the earliest of the prophets writing around 830 B.C. during the reign of Joash.

II. The Contemporaries of the Prophet: No other writing-prophet ministered during the ministry of Joel. Elisha may have been a prophetic contemporary.

III. The Theme of the Book: The theme of the Book of Joel is "The Day of the Lord."

IV. The Key Verses of the Book: " 'Yet even now,' declares the Lord, 'Return to me with all your heart, and with fasting, weeping, and mourning; and rend your heart and not your garments.' Now return to the Lord your God, for He is generous and compassionate, slow to anger, abounding in lovingkindness, and relenting of evil." (2:12-13)

V. Background Reading: 2 Chronicles 24:1-27

Joel is one of the earliest of the Minor Prophets. His prophecy, probably written during the reign of Joash in Judah, spans a broad spectrum of time from local events that afflicted the nation during his lifetime to an announcement of those events which would mark the end of this age. The Book of Joel has been described as one of the literary gems of the Bible. Carson, in *The New Bible Commentary,* describes Joel, saying, "It is built with care and dramatic effect; here and there throughout its chapters are beauties which shine brilliantly and even dazzle the imagination."

The Book of Joel holds a peculiar relevance to our day. The prophet spoke of current problems that had touched the lives of virtually every strata of Judean society. A "shrinking" globe has demanded mutual dependency as never before in this half of the twentieth century. It has not been unusual to see national and international difficulties arise that can change the course of people's lives and create political and economic problems of an unparalleled character. "It is at a time such as these," writes Frederick Tatford in *Prophet of the Judgment Day,* "that the burden of temporal care weighs heavily and faith too often fails. Yet, if true religion means anything at all, it is surely at such times that we should be able to prove its reality." J. H. Kennedy appropriately remarks:

> National disasters and human sufferings have always made special demands upon thoughtful and responsible men. These experiences often become unique occasions for serious, even ultimate questions. The Book of Joel is the record of one such calamity and the consequent human sufferings. It is also the witness to a meaningful interpretation of that crisis furnished through the spiritual resources of a man of faith. Accordingly, the book has a timeless quality of point and pertinence for every generation and for every new experience of deep distress."

Nothing is known of the author of this prophecy and the book itself contains no direct information regarding his background, character or occupation. His message was concerned solely with Judah. Joel, however, looks beyond the situation of his day to the glories and blessings of the millennial age.

The Theme of the Book

Joel, like Obadiah and Zephaniah, emphasizes the *Day of the Lord.* Five times in the book, reference is made to this *period of time when God personally intervenes in the affairs of men in judgment.* It is this term and the amplification of it through historical instances that make up the theme of the book.

The Current Catastrophe

Joel's prophecy begins with a vivid description of a catastrophe that was afflicting the people of Judah. The unprecedented disaster was of such intensity that Joel turned to the eldest of his countrymen to ask whether their experience held any recollection of an occurrence so dreadful (1:2-3). The text suggests that the locust plague to which Joel refers had descended upon the land in successive years (2:25) causing special burdens upon every strata of society. Joel 1:16 implies that a plague was being experienced at the time of Joel's ministry.

The plague was one of locusts who had descended upon the land and caused unparalleled chaos to the land of Judah. The awful devastation caused by such an invasion is difficult to comprehend. *The Encyclopedia Britannica* says:

> The size and destructiveness of a large locust swarm are tremendous. Many cover 100 square miles while in flight; some have been estimated to cover as much as 2,000 square miles. It has been reliably reported that the total coverage of the desert locust swarms that invaded Kenya in January 1954 was 500 square miles. An outbreak of desert locusts weighing approximately 50,000 tons and eating their own weight in green vegetation daily while growing or migrating occurred in Somalia in 1957. Migrations usually are with the wind and aided by it. . . . Some flights are near the ground, others more than a mile above it. Flying with the wind is advantageous to the locust because air currents that aid in transportation often drop rain, creating a congenial breeding ground where the swarm settles.

Frequently an invasion of locusts is likened unto an uncontained brush fire; the huge swarms of insects actually darken the sun and the noise of their wings crackles like the sound of a consuming fire.

Joel described the swarm of locusts by four names and declared that what one had left, the next had devoured (1:4). Pusey in his book of *The Minor Prophets* says there were over 80 species of locusts in Palestine, all possessing insatiable appetites capable of causing total devastation to vegetation. The four terms Joel uses to describe the insects that afflicted Judah were: *gazam* (shearer), *'arbeh* (swarmer), *yelek* (lapper), and *hasil* (stripper). With teeth like lions (1:6) they moved throughout the land like a mighty army leaving total ruin in their wake.

Differing views have arisen as to the significance of the prophet's description. Some have suggested that the names used by Joel relate to different stages of growth among locusts; while others have contended that at least four successive invasions had occurred in succeeding years. Perhaps there had already been four swarms and Judah now awaited with dread expectancy for a fifth. It is interesting that the prophet mentions *four* insects which were devouring Judah and Daniel later describes four beasts (nations) that would "devour" Judah (Babylon, Medo-Persia, Greece and Rome).

The disaster to which Joel refers afflicted everyone from the drunkard (1:5) to the priest (1:9). The famine which resulted brought untold misery to the entire population of Judah (1:16-18). For God to direct an army of locusts (2:11, 25) that would touch agriculture was a blow that disrupted not only daily life in Judah, but it also disrupted the entire economic foundation of that society.

The plague provided opportunity for Judah to repent and again recognize God as their only source of strength and sustenance (2:12-13). God is seen frequently working in the prophets (cf. Amos 4:6-11) in "preliminary" ways seeking to bring men to a recognition of their need of Him. These encounters, short of total destruction, were often unheeded. Men of today, like of old, need the spiritual perception to discern God's working in their day!

The Day of the Lord

There have been times during the course of history that the sins of men became so intolerable to God that He personally intervened in terrible judgment. The flood during the days of Noah is one such period. The Genesis record indicates that "the earth was corrupt in the sight of God and . . . filled with violence" (Gen. 6:12). Wickedness on the earth was so great that even the idle time of men in Noah's day was given to the preparation of wicked deeds (Gen. 6:5). God was grieved at what He saw and purposed in His plan to judge the world by a universal flood. Even in judgment an opportunity to repent was provided through the faithful testimony of Noah and his godly family whom the Lord graciously preserved.

The phrase "the day of the Lord" is a synonym for "the day of judgment," or the "time of divine judgment." It is reserved in its use to periods of extraordinary intervention by God. Girdlestone writes in his book entitled *The Grammar of Prophecy* as follows:

> This expression had to do with the fall of Babylon (Isa. 13:6), when the punishment of Egypt (Ezek. 30:3), and with the destruction of Israel and Jerusalem (Joel 1:15; Zeph. 1:7, 14, 18). Similar expressions, which refer to temporal judgments may be noted in Isaiah 13:9, Joel 2:1 and Zechariah 14:1. These passages throw light on kindred utterances in the New Testament, and justify us in looking upon the fall of Jerusalem (A.D. 70) as a special manifestation of the day of the Lord; though the full force of the expression is yet in the future.

There are four special features of the use of this phrase that deserve special attention.

The Day of the Lord is not one specific period of time. This phrase is not principally a reference to one specific period of time. It *always* refers to a time of judgment. The term is *never* used in the Bible to describe a period of bless-ing, as is sometimes taught. The day of His judgment, the "day of the Lord," is *any* day when God is judging.

The day of the Lord may refer to cases of impending tem-poral judgment. In the prophecy of Joel, the locust plague is used in chapters 1 and 2 as an example of the day of the Lord.

The day of the Lord is frequently prophetically announced. In the case of the captivities of Israel, God prepared men to deliver a message of imminent judgment. Their message fre-quently fell on deafened ears, but God remained faithful in providing an opportunity for repentance. The Scriptures pro-vide for men today a solemn warning of the judgment yet to come with a gracious provision made for all men to repent and trust the Lord Jesus Christ.

The day of the Lord most frequently refers to the con-summating judgments that will attend our Lord's second coming. The Apostle Paul wrote in 2 Thessalonians that (1) the removal of "that which restraineth" (2 Thess. 2:6-7), and (2) the revelation of the man of sin (2 Thess. 2:3-4) must precede the day of the Lord. In this context the "day of the Lord" is used to refer to the final judgments, including the period of judgment after the millennial reign of our Lord (2 Peter 3:10). There may be some passages where it refers to the judgments of the Tribulation period.

Joel provides a panoramic picture of the day of the Lord. The idea of a temporal manifestation of God's judgment is seen in the locust plague. A more prophetic fulfillment of the descriptions in the book, especially chapter 2, is seen by some commentators as predicting a forthcoming invasion of Assyria over Israel. William Kelly in his *Lectures Introduc-tory to the Study of the Minor Prophets* adopts this position when writing:

> Joel uses the present visitation as a fact, but withal employs language which forms an easy passage to the prediction of a nation that would deal with the Jews in an unparalleled way. There need be no doubt that the nation in question is the As-

syrian. The first chapter starts with the repeated and frightful depredations of the locusts in the prophet's day, but looks on to the trouble of a terrible day. The second chapter directly notices no such havoc from insects, but mingles figures taken from them with the Assyrian who should surely come up.

The final segment of the book (2:28—3:21) establishes the program of the day of the Lord yet to be fulfilled.

There is much that can be learned about God through a study of His actions. One of the great principles of God's dealings with mankind is observed by Charles Feinberg in his commentary *Joel, Amos and Obadiah.* He writes: "God only inflicts punishment after great provocation, and when He does so, it is meant to draw man back from further and more severe visitations of the wrath of God."

The Promises for the Future

There is no doubt that Joel speaks of events that would take place long after his personal ministry. The prophet speaks of three specific events that deserve special attention.

The outpouring of the Spirit (2:28-29). Joel prophesied that there would be a time when God would pour out His spirit upon all flesh. The promise is introduced by the expression, "*It shall be afterwards,*" creating some confusion as to exactly what the prophet referred to that would precede this outpouring of the Spirit of God.

Frederick Tatford suggests that this expression is to be understood, not with the circumstances of Joel's time, but with the latter days (Hosea 3:5). Others, however, observe a transition in the message of the prophet and see an earlier reference to a battle that will take place during the first half of the Great Tribulation. Dr. Charles Smith writes: "When they [Israel] repent during the first half of the tribulation during the Northerner's oppression, then *after that,* Jehovah will pour out His spirit upon them."

In any case it seems apparent that the events of Pentecost were not a complete fulfillment of Joel's prophecy. Tatford recognizes the problem when writing:

It is frequently stated that the apostle Peter expressly claimed that the descent of the Holy Spirit at Pentecost was the fulfillment of Joel's prophecy (Acts 2:16-21), but the accompanying details, which the apostle quoted, were not, of course, fulfilled at Pentecost. Peter merely implied that what had transpired at Pentecost was of the same nature as the events foretold by Joel, and it is obvious that the complete fulfillment awaits the outpouring of the Holy Spirit in the millennium (Ezek. 39:29).

The Final Judgment upon the nations (3:1). Joel proceeds in his message to describe a time when God would deal appropriately with those nations who had mistreated the people of Israel. The prophet indicates that the nations would be gathered together for judgment in the Valley of Jehosaphat (The Valley of Jehovah's Judgment) after Israel had been restored to the land. The charges against the nation are leveled by God (3:4-8) after which a proclamation of war is heralded (3:9-10). The ensuing battle will be a dramatic expression of God's love for Israel and His animosity to those who have despised her. The Day of the Lord is seen here in its ultimate fulfillment.

The Final Blessings (3:18, 20-21). The land originally promised to Israel was to be "a good land . . . flowing with milk and honey" (Exod. 3:8). *Every* promise to Israel will be fulfilled in perfect detail when the nation is eventually established in their own land in the millennium.

The Desired Response

The Book of Joel looks beyond the present scourge of locusts afflicting Judah and envisions the entire program of God which culminates in the final warfare between God and the gentile nations. The rebellious hearts of the people of Judah prompted the prophet to plead for their repentance (2:12-14). The Lord besought them to "Return to Me with all your hearts" indicating that there must be a deliberate resolution on their behalf to turn their back upon the sin that characterized their way of life and to show their allegiance to God.

Certainly the message of this hour ought to be the same! If ever there was a time when men ought to "rend their hearts and not their garments," it is today. On the subject of repentance, Jeremy Taylor (*The Minor Prophets*) writes: "Although all sorrow for sin has not the same expression, nor the same degree of pungency and sensitive trouble, yet it is not a godly sorrow unless it produces these effects: (1) that it makes us to really hate; and (2) actually to decline to sin; and (3) produces in us a fear of God's anger, a sense of the guilt of His displeasure . . . ." Frederick Tatford concurs, when he says:

"True repentance does not consist of sloppy sentimentality or in empty and meaningless phraseology, but in a heartfelt remorse and a sincere and deliberate change of attitude. . . . It might be of great spiritual value if the supercilious superficiality of the present was exposed for its unreality and artificiality, and the torment of transgression again realized in all its heart-rending grief!"

If the people of Joel's time had unreservedly abandoned their sinful habits and wicked practices, God would have been gracious and merciful to them. Would God do less today?

3

Amos: Israel Out of Plumb

KEYS THAT UNLOCK AMOS

I.   The Time of the Book: Amos is a pre-exilic prophet to Israel.

II. The Contemporaries of the Prophet: Those prophets that ministered around the same time as Amos include: Hosea and Jonah.

III. The Theme of the Book: The theme of the book is "The Justice of God."

IV. The Key Verse of the Book: "But let justice roll down like waters, and righteousness like an ever-flowing stream" (Amos 5:24).

V.   Background Reading: 2 Kings 14–20; 2 Chronicles 26–32

Of all those called of God to prophesy, Amos might well have appeared the most unlikely. Little of his background is known to us other than that revealed in the book that bears his name. Unlike other prophets whose lineage and credentials preface their message, this prophet identifies himself as only a "sheepherder" and a "grower of sycamore figs" (7:14) from Tekoa, a tiny village six miles south of Bethlehem in an area belonging to Judah (2 Chron. 11:6). He was untrained as a prophet (7:14), preeminently a man of the wilderness.

It was to this man that God spoke and revealed His message of impending doom upon the prosperous and unsuspecting nation of Israel. His message was bold, characterized as one of "great rhetorical power" and rich in its "poetic expression." There seems to have been no positive response to its demands. So enraged by the implications of his proclamations, Amaziah the high priest of Bethel (7:12-17), went to Israel's King Jeroboam pronouncing Amos as a traitor. The subsequent denunciation of Amaziah by Amos (7:16-17) has led to the tradition that the prophet died as a consequence of this high priest's brutality. While the Scriptures are silent as to Amos' end, such a reaction is not out of character to that which might have been anticipated.

The ministry of Amos took place "in the days of Uzziah, King of Judah, and in the days of Jeroboam son of Joash, king of Israel . . ." (1:1). This would make him a contemporary with Hosea, Isaiah, Jonah and probably Micah. Amos could have been pronouncing judgment upon Israel at the hands of the Assyrians at the same time Jonah was preaching repentance to the inhabitants of the Assyrian capital of Nineveh! The prophets clearly reveal that Jehovah is Lord of all!

The Theme of the Book

The Book of Amos presents an indisputable case for the absolute necessity for divine judgment. God had graciously provided the nation Israel with numerous opportunities to repent, all of which had passed unheeded (4:6-11). The time now had come for direct intervention. Through a series of three discourses (3:1-6, 14) and five visions (7:1—9:10) the impending judgment upon Israel is presented as totally just. The nation had repeatedly forsaken the righteous standards of God. In his book titled *Amos: The Prophet of Social Justice,* P. H. Kelley writes that this book reveals that "God's rule extends to all nations and that the standard by which the nations are judged is the standard of absolute justice." *The justice of God is the theme of the Book of Amos.*

The Scene

The casual visitor to Israel during the days of Amos would have been impressed. Outwardly the nation flourished. Gaebelein called this time "the golden age" of Israel's history. It was a period generally characterized by great wealth and luxury, arrogant pride and self-security. A more penetrating look, however, would reveal a society that was internally corrupt, based upon an eroding foundation of greed. The deterioration of meaningful values spelled the dreadful judgment of the nation; a message prophesied by the ragged prophet from Tekoa.

The Book of Amos focuses upon particular characteristics of the Israel to which the prophet had been called. The noteworthy would include the following:

It was a period of unparalleled prosperity (3:10, 15; 4:3; 5:11; 6:1, 4). Special attention is given by the prophet to the extravagances of Israel's wealthy. Many had both summer and winter homes (3:15) that were magnificently appointed. They were at ease, comforted by a temporary political stability. They pampered themselves (6:3-6), completely oblivious to their dire spiritual need.

Of these extravagances Tatford has written:

It was not their wealth or their enjoyment of the material benefits of life which the prophet criticized, but rather the methods by which they had been acquired and the attitudes they displayed towards them. The Bible does not demand asceticism or prohibit the enjoyment of the blessings God bestows, provided there is the true spirit of thankfulness to the One who is the donor of it all. But a practice of unreserved self-indulgence at the expense of others or in the presence of others' needs is well deserving of the strictures of Amos. Yet such heedless hedonism is not entirely missing today. One part of the world starves, while another lives in affluence.

It was a period of political stability (2 Kings 14:23-29). In his commentary titled *Amos,* J. L. Mays writes:

> The background of Israel's self-congratulation lay in the remarkable resurgence of national power which Israel had experienced under Jeroboam II. With his constant adversary, Damascus, crippled by Assyrian campaigning, Jeroboam had been able to recoup Israel's previous losses east of Jordan; 2 Kings 14:25 implies that Jeroboam had recovered all the territory in that quarter which Israel had ever held.

Israel freely boasted of their accomplishments, wrought in their own strength. Writes Keil:

> In the existing state of things the idea of the approaching fall or destruction of the kingdom of Israel was, according to human judgment, a very improbable one indeed. The inhabitants of Samaria and Zion felt themselves perfectly secure in the consciousness of their might (6:1). The rulers of the kingdom trusted in the strength of their military resources (6:13).

It was a period of social irresponsibility (5:7). Laced throughout the Book of Amos are references to the social abuses of the wealthy aristocracy upon the helpless poor. The rich arrogantly glorified in their opulence while the impoverished suffered. It seems evident from later portions of the prophecy that there was no longer a consciousness of wrongdoing on the part of the privileged. The picture that is so vividly painted by the prophet is one of heartless oppression.

Inequities had spawned in every area of life and never to the advantage of the underprivileged. The nation had turned justice into a bitter experience and the concepts of righteousness and fair play were totally meaningless (5:7). God pleaded through Amos to the nation, "But let justice roll on like waters and righteousness as a perennial stream" (5:24). On this pivotal key verse of the book, McFayden comments:

These are immortal words; they express in imperishable form the essence of religion, the simple demands of God upon man. The justice, the righteousness for which Amos here pleads is . . . a social thing: it is a tender regard for the poor, hatred of the evil conditions that have dwarfed their lives (5:15); it is the spirit that yearns and works for the removal of these conditions; it is, in a word, respect for personality, fair play as between man and man. Let justice, in that sense, run through society, unimpeded by avarice or selfishness or cruelty, let it roll on without hindrance like the waves of the sea; let it roll on unintermittently, all the year round, whatever be the political weather; let it roll on "like a perennial stream," which even in the fiercest heat of summer never dries up.

It was a period of religious corruption (2:7; 4:4; 5:4, 21-23). Israel professed extraordinary zeal for God's worship by their punctilious observance of religious requirements. They made their annual pilgrimages on the festival occasions and declared through their offerings their commitment to the Lord. To their astonished ears Amos pronounced that God rejected their religious practices (5:21-23). As Patterson says in his book *The Goodly Fellowship of the Prophets*, "The ethnic of the thing done had been substituted for the ethic of the clean heart; religion had become externalized and materialized."

It was a period of domestic erosion (4:1-3). It is likely that no pronouncement of Amos brought more negative reaction than his bold proclamation to the upper-class ladies of Samaria, "Hear this word, you cows of Bashan . . ." (4:1). Writes Tatford:

The prophet described these sleek, well-fed women, who spent their days in voluptuous dalliance or indolent *ennui*, as cows of Bashan, who lived in the hill country of Samaria. Bashan was noted for the excellence of its cattle: its rich pastures in the east of Jordan produced the fattest and strongest animals (Deut.

32:24; Ps. 22:12), and they were used as a symbol of the mighty (Ezek. 39:18). It was an appropriate simile for these female Sybarites, whose hedonism was apparent to all...." It mattered nothing to them, even if they were aware of it, that their luxuries were continually watered by tears of the power.

The constant demands upon their husbands resulted in incredible abuses. Women had gained illegitimate control and influence in the home. This erosion of the family unit contributed to the fall of an entire nation!

Amos has frequently been called "The Prophet of Social Justice" because such a large portion of his message concerns the social evils in Israel. But Amos' approach and solution was different from modern "social workers" and social psychologists. Many of these feel that the problem is strictly man-to-man relationships. They completely misunderstand the Bible emphasis. Dale Carnegie said: "The ideas I stand for are not mine, I borrowed them from Socrates, I swiped them from Chesterfield, I stole them from Jesus, and I put them in a book. If you do not like 'their' rules, whose would you use?" But *Christ* realized, as Amos also proclaimed, that the basic problem was not strictly man-to-man relationships, but the man-to-*God* relationship!

The Nature of the Judgment

Amos' message was a stunning blow to those who listened (7:10-13). The unpretentious prophet boldly proclaimed his message in words that betrayed his humble background. As Patterson remarks: "The wide open spaces in which he [Amos] lived are reflected in the amplitude of his spiritual vision . . . all his similes and metaphors reflect the bare gaunt background of the desert." It was to the sophisticated capital city of Samaria that the prophet came. The huge city, built on a hill nearly 300 feet high and almost completely surrounded by much higher mountains, was the pride of Israel. Its streets bustled with activity, its inhabitants secure in their prosperity and shocked by the herdsman who prophesied judgment and destruction. Three unsavory announcements are made by Amos concerning the future retribution from God.

God had repeatedly warned the nation (4:6-11). These verses contain a detailed record of the catastrophes God brought upon Israel for the specific purpose of arousing them to a realization of their dependence upon Him. The five calamities were: famine (4:6), drought (4:7-8), crop failure (4:9), pestilence (4:10) and earthquake (4:11). Each of the accounts ends with the sad phrase, "Yet you did not return to me."

Severer judgment had been mercifully withheld (7:1-6). The first two visions which mark the concluding section of the book relate that God had mercifully withheld more severe judgments. God revealed to the prophet that locusts would swarm upon the land at the crucial harvest season and devour everything in their sight. Such an event would confront Israel with imminent famine, jeopardizing their very existence.

Amos acted as an intercessor on behalf of the people and pleaded with God to forgive the nation (7:2). God relented in His plan.

A second vision of fire sweeping across the Israeli countryside, licking up the water and devastating the land was shown the prophet. Again Amos intervened and a second time the Lord repented and declared that it should not happen. Of this repentance of God, R. L. Smith (*The Broadman Bible Commentary*) writes: "Repentance, when it is used of God, does not include any sense of sin, error or wrongdoing on the part of God. It does suggest perhaps a sense of sorrow that judgment has been necessary. It is an anthropopathism frequently used by the Scripture writers."

Israel would eventually be stunned by a great military conquest (3:11, 14:15; 6:8, 11). Despite all of God's gracious warnings and pleas in the past, Israel was adamant in her sin. Amos proclaimed that punishment would eventually fall, not merely upon the nation for its transgression but upon the very center of their religion. This would involve the destruction of their cities and the monuments to their greed (3:16), incredible human suffering (6:9-10) and captivity for the survivors (5:27).

The nation of Israel undoubtedly rejoiced in the initial announcements of doom by Amos upon her neighbors (Amos 1–2). These nations were limited in their understanding of God, but they were held completely responsible to Him for their behavior. In his commentary *The Minor Prophets*, Jeremy Taylor writes that "Men do not have to know the full revelation of God's law to come under His condemnation: They only have to violate the standards that they, in their relatively unenlightened state, can yet recognize (cf. Rom. 1:18-30; 2:12)." If *they* were accountable to the Sovereign of the Universe for their conduct, how much more the responsibility for a nation privileged above all, elect of all the families of the earth (3:1-2).

The Necessity of Judgment

Two of the five visions that conclude the Book of Amos unmistakably illustrate the absolute *necessity* for divine judgment. Any doubt was forever settled as a holy and just God stood before a wall in a vision to Amos and demonstratively showed Israel far removed from the righteous standards of God.

"Thus he showed me, and behold, the Lord was standing by a vertical wall, with a plumb line in His hand. And the Lord said to me, 'What do you see, Amos?' And I said, 'A plumbline.' Then the Lord said, 'Behold I am about to put a plumbline in the midst of My people Israel. I will spare them no longer' " (7:8-9).

The plumb is a carpenter's tool. The line it establishes is perfectly perpendicular. It is an unquestionable guide that enables one to see what his eye might not be able to judge accurately.

The problem with crooked things is that the longer you live with them, the more prone they are to look normal. Israel had perverted justice for so long that it had become a way of life. Everyone would rather judge themselves by another and so rationalize away their own wickedness. You can always find someone worse off than yourself! In evaluating ourselves, however, we are to look to those things that are absolute, that change not. The righteous and holy character of God is a safe plumb line that, when set beside our lives, should challenge us to purity.

The Israel (represented by the wall) in Amos' vision was dangerously "out of plumb," far removed from the righteous character and demands of God.

In another vision, *"The Lord showed me [Amos] . . . a basket of summer fruit. And He said, 'What do you see, Amos?' And I said, 'A basket of summer fruit.' Then the Lord said to me, 'The end has come for My people Israel. I will spare them no longer!' "* (8:1-2).

The significance of the vision was explained by the Lord. Just as the contents of the basket indicated the harvest had ended, so the end had come for the nation Israel. They were ripe for judgment. Their sin could no longer be passed over. It was too late now for penitence. The end had come!

Mercy Amidst Judgment

One of the special features of the Old Testament prophets are their messages of hope. An organization of these promises alone will provide an interesting and rewarding study. Amos is no exception as the final verses of this book (9:11-15) provide Israel with the assurance that God cares and has an eternal plan for them. Included in that plan will be the restoration of the Davidic empire (9:11), a time of unparalleled blessing (9:13), a full restoration of the nation to its land (9:14) and the guarantee that this habitation will be permanent (9:15).

The kingdom was to fall but God would raise it again! These promises extend beyond Israel to include the nation Judah. They would again be united as in the days of David. The phrase, "days of old" (9:11) implies that a long period will elapse between the fall and rising again.

Conclusion

It has been said that "the wheels of God's justice move slowly but grind exceedingly smooth." Since the dividing of the kingdom in the days of Jeroboam, God had allowed the nation Israel to persist in their sin, graciously providing them numerous opportunities to again place their trust totally upon Him. For over 200 years they refused. It would be the Assyrians now who would act as the chastening instruments of God. Their armies would devastate Israel and take survivors captive, just as Amos had prophesied. The scriptural injunction, *"Be not deceived, God is not mocked; whatsoever a man soweth, that shall he also reap"* (Gal. 6:7) is as true among nations as it is among men!

4

Obadiah: The Fall of Edom

KEYS THAT UNLOCK OBADIAH

I. The Time of the Book: Obadiah is a pre-exilic prophet from Israel with a special message to Edom.

II. The Contemporaries of Obadiah: No other writing-prophet ministered during the time of Obadiah. Elisha may have been a prophetic contemporary.

III. The Theme of the Book: "Jehovah: Lord Over All"

IV. The Key Verse of the Book: "For the day of the Lord draws near on all the nations. As you have done, it will be done to you. Your dealings will return on your own head" (verse 15).

V. Background Reading:
   Ezekiel 35:1-15
   Isaiah 63:1-19
   Numbers 20:14-21
   Jeremiah 49:7-22
   Isaiah 34:1-17

Israel owns a special place in the heart of God. The nations of the world will eventually be judged on the basis of their attitude to God's chosen people. The brief prophecy of Obadiah demonstrates these truths quite graphically as the prophet declares unmitigated condemnation upon the descendants of Esau, the nation of Edom.

The unique character of Obadiah was observed by George Adam Smith in his book *The Book of the Twelve Prophets* when he wrote of Obadiah that "it brings no spiritual message. It speaks no word of sin, or of righteousness, or of mercy, but only doom upon Edom in bitter resentment at his cruelties, and in exultation that, as he has helped to disinherit Israel, Israel shall disinherit him." The book clearly intimates that God is ultimately sovereign in the affairs of all men, even those who clearly exclude Him from their way of life.

It was for the wrongs inflicted by Edom upon Israel which led to the outpouring of the prophet's denunciation. God's wrath would be unreserved. These descendants of Esau are the recipients of several messages from God in the Scriptures. Floyd E. Hamilton has categorized the revelation concerning Edom's future in his book *The Basis of Christian Faith.* He writes:

> There are four remarkable prophecies about Edom ... that have been fulfilled. The first of these four prophecies concern the trade. "I will cut off from it him that passeth through and him that returneth" (Ezek. 35:7). The trade of the country was to cease and the caravans were to travel through the country no more. At the time this was written, nothing seemed more improbable of fulfillment than this prophecy, yet today great silence reigns over the ruins of these old market towns and the caravan is never seen passing through the country, where formerly thousands of people passed each year.
>
> The second prophecy concerned the people themselves. "There shall not be left any remaining to the house of Esau" (Oba. 18). The people were to be wholly destroyed and utterly wiped out. This prophecy, likewise, seemed most strange, for the

people of Edom were almost as numerous as the people of Israel, and the Jews remain today a distinct and separate people. None can be pointed out as definitely of Edomite descent today.

A still stranger prophecy was that the land itself should be desolate. "Behold I am against thee, O Mount Seir, and I will stretch out my hand against thee, and I will make thee a desolation and an astonishment. I will lay thy cities waste and thou shalt be desolate" (Ezek. 35:3-4). Other lands have had their people cut off, but are still inhabited; why should we not expect that Edom would be the same? . . . Yet today the cities are deserted, and the cliff homes of Edom are without human habitation.

But perhaps the most remarkable of all is a prophecy which foretells the very town from which the limitation of the desolation was to be set. "I will make it desolate from Teman" (Ezek. 35:13). And strange as it may seem, Teman or Maan . . . is still a prosperous town . . . and the only city in all that land that is not deserted.

Organization of the Book

The Book of Obadiah and its brief 21 verses are rich in their revelation of God and His dealings with men. Pusey's verse by verse analysis tells the story of the book in a rather concise manner and is worth review. He writes that

God had commanded nations to come against Edom (1) determining to lower it (2). Edom had trusted proudly in its strong position (3) yet God would bring it down (4) and that through no ordinary spoiler (5) but by one who would search out its most hidden treasures (6). Its friends would be its destroyers (7). Its wisdom (8) and might (9) should fail it, and it should perish for its malice to its brother Jacob (10); the crowning act of which would be at the capture of Jerusalem (11-14). But God's day was at hand, the heathen would be requited (15-16). The remnant of Zion, being delivered, would dispossess their possessions, and would spread far and wide (17-20). A Saviour would arise out of Zion, and the kingdom should be the Lord's (21).

J. Sidlow Baxter calls Obadiah "The Prophet of Poetic Justice" and divides the book in two major sections: The Destruction of Edom (1-16) and the Salvation of Israel (17-21).

It shall be around these two messages that our thoughts will be centered.

The Destruction of Edom

The Edomites were the descendants of Esau who occupied the hill country south of the Dead Sea. Despite their close relationship to the Israelites, Esau's descendants were the ruthless enemies of the people of God. This hatred of Israel is continually evidenced throughout the Old Testament. During the periods of the exodus, Moses sought permission to pass through Edom's territory only to receive a resounding refusal and a threat to use arms if any violation of Edom's territorial rights occurred (Num. 20:14-21). There were successive attacks upon Edom by both Saul (1 Sam. 14:47) and David (2 Sam. 8:14) before the nation received its independence during the days of Jehoram (2 Kings 8:20-22).

The Edomite territory was known for its unassailable security. Nelson Glueck wrote of the land that "practically every site throughout the length and breath of the land consisted either of a great fortress or a strong blockhouse." The nation was notorious for its pride and arrogance. Their cities were considered impregnable, no foe was feared!

This writer recently visited the ancient city of Petra, the Edomite capital, and was astounded. The only entrance into the city is a narrow gorge between towering cliffs 200 to 300 feet tall. A handful of men could undoubtedly protect this entrance against any invading army. The path twists and turns amidst the cliffs for over a mile until suddenly and unexpectedly you are confronted by the facade of a building carved out of the rock. This building, commonly referred to as the Treasury, is but one of the many marvelous sights to be seen within the city. There are still remains of a giant theatre which once accommodated 2,000 people. A visitor to Petra can still see the ruins of the triumphal arch, the market place, an old temple and palace. As we left the city on our horses there was little doubt left that overcoming the occupants of this city had to be ordered and directed by God!

Obadiah bears the message of Jehovah (v. 1) in announcing that the chastisement previously threatened by the prophets (Isa. 21:1-10) was about to be inflicted. The "apple of God's eye" (Zech. 2:8) had been violated arousing His righteous indignation. There is a sense of urgency with which Obadiah states his case. Judgment was imminent!

The prominent theme of Obadiah's prophecy, as already expressed, is the destruction of Edom. The underlying basis for this righteous act was the behavior of the nation especially as it related to the nation of Israel. The abiding biblical principle that is clearly in evidence here and throughout Scripture, "whatsoever a man soweth, that shall he also reap" (Gal. 6:7), is equally as applicable to the nations of the world as it is individuals. A review of the destruction prophesied here deserves the consideration of the following:

The prevailing attitudes of Edom. Solomon declared that "pride goes before destruction, and a haughty spirit before a fall" (Prov. 16:18). The boastful arrogance of Edom was based on the rationale that their cities were beyond military reach. They defiantly rejected God in favor of their own strength and position! Obadiah's message that they would be brought down (4) was incomprehensible to the haughty nation.

Stubborn men have pursued similar tactics in our day. Through massive armament expenditures, nations have considered themselves invulnerable from hostile forces. Our nation prides itself in its "inner strength" and "national pride" and looks with almost cultic devotion to the victories of the past. Could it be that while we are defiantly raising our fist to the world and saying "Just try something!" that God looks down and pleads for men to simply put their trust in Him? There is a delusion in pride; men lose their objectivity and that was certainly the case with Edom. The prophet declares that the arrogance of their heart had deceived them (v. 3).

Not only was the nation condemned for its arrogance, but

also more specifically for its continual display of hostility toward the nation Israel. The prophets clearly declare that even God's people are not exempt from His wrath. A time would come when both Israel and Judah would be crushed by the invader because of their rebellion against the revelation of God. Edom was warned, however, not to "gloat" and "rejoice" (vv. 12-13) in this calamity for, despite the prevailing situation, God intended to fulfill His commitment to His people. It is that reality, the absolute faithfulness of God to His promises, that is the basis of our hermeneutic. This is the present hope of Israel and of all those who today embrace the substitutionary provision of Christ. We rest in the assurance that God will complete His work in us. Edom was condemned because of rebellion against the plan, program, and people of God.

The manner of destruction. Details of the destruction of Edom are included in Obadiah's announcement. Isaac was foretold (Gen. 27:40) that Edom would live to a great extent by the sword. One has written of the Edomites that, "By the sword they got Mount Seir, by the sword they exterminated the Horites, by the sword they battled with the brethren of Israel and finally broke off their yoke, by the sword they won southern Palestine, and by the sword they performed the last act in their long historic drama, massacred the guards in the temple and pillaged the city of Jerusalem." Now, according to the prophet, they were to suffer by the sword.

The judgment that is pronounced here fulfills the prediction of Jeremiah that "Edom shall be a desolation" (Jer. 49:17). Ewald writes that

Everyone who considers the character of this calamity must come to the conclusion that a higher hand is here at work. For if this had been a common attack, like those which nomadic nations are accustomed to make, Edom would not have been so completely plundered, or as barbarously treated; thieves steal only as much as seems good to them, vine dressers similarly always leave at least a gleaning: but alas, how is Edom utterly destroyed, completely robbed and ransacked!

The nation would become a complete shambles. The astonishment of Obadiah is justified when he proclaimed, "How complete is your destruction!" (v. 5).

Poetic justice is what J. Sidlow Baxter calls the judgment of Edom. He writes that

Edom had indulged in treachery against Judah (verses 11-12); therefore Edom should perish through the treachery of confederates (verse 7). Edom had seized the change to rob Judah (verse 13); therefore Edom should be robbed even till his hidden things, or treasures, were searched out (verses 5, 6). Edom had lifted the sword and shown violence against Judah (verse 10); therefore Edom should perish by slaughter (verse 9). Edom had sought the utter destruction of Judah (verses 12-14); therefore Edom should be utterly destroyed (verses 10, 18). Edom had even sought to hand over and dispossess the remnant of the invaded Jerusalem (verse 14); therefore, in the end, the remnant of Jacob should possess the land of Edom (verse 19). The very extermination of Edom is prophesied by Obadiah. The long accumulating guilt of the nation would be finally judged!

The Salvation of Israel

The concluding verses of this shortest book in the Old Testament speak of the future restoration and blessing of Israel. The corrective chastening of the nation's past did not cancel God's covenant promises. Throughout history God has preserved this special nation. One writer has suggested that the initial clause of verse 17, "But in Mount Zion there will be those who escape" depicts a "successive flow of this stream of salvation. Generation upon generation may come and go, and each will find salvation on Mount Zion (Isaiah 33:20-24; Lamatations 3:22-ff)."

Among the special features to be noted of this final restoration, the following deserve special consideration:

Israel will possess her possessions (v. 17). A time will come when the nation will enjoy her possessions. God has bound Himself irrevocably to fulfill His covenants. Among those covenant promises was a land, the borders of which are given specifically in Genesis 15:18-21. At no time in history has Israel occupied the breadth of the land promised here by God. The prophets anticipated a time when a united nation, "the house of Jacob," would take possession of the whole of the land of promise!

Israel will be ruled by divinely appointed leaders (v. 21). This is the consummation of all that is anticipated. God is viewed as the Supreme Ruler. Perowne writes in his commentary on Obadiah:

> It is this that stamps the writings of the Hebrew prophets with a character which is all their own, and proves them to be inspired with an inspiration of God, other and higher far than that of the most gifted seers and poets of other lands and ages. With them the rational and the human reach forth ever to the divine and the universal. The kingdom of Israel gives place to and is lost in the kingdom of God. . . . Still Obadiah's last note of prophecy vibrates on, till at last it shall be taken up into the great chorus of accomplished hope and satisfied expectation, "Hallelujah! for the Lord God omnipotent reigneth!"

Thus ends this "remarkable fragment from the pen of Obadiah." The tiny prophecy speaks anew of God and His dealings with men. Perhaps the words of A. T. Pierson provide an ample conclusion to this intriguing study:

> Whatever had to do with God is, of necessity and in the nature of things, supernatural and superhuman, extra-ordinary and unique. It belongs on a level of its own, standing alone and part, by itself, unapproachable, defying alike competition and comparison. We should therefore expect both sublimity and originality, elevation and isolation, much that transcends all the limits of human thought, involving more or less the element of the inscrutable: and the presence of such characteristics instead of an obstacle to faith is rather an argument for it.

God's program goes forward. The Kingdom *is* the Lord's!

5

Jonah: The Prophet Who Ran Away

KEYS THAT UNLOCK JONAH

I.   The Time of the Book: Jonah was a pre-exilic prophet from Israel with a special message to Nineveh.

II. The Contemporaries of Jonah: Amos may have been a contemporary of the prophet Jonah.

III. The Theme of the Book: The Mercy of God

IV. The Key Verse of the Book: "But I will sacrifice to Thee with the voice of thanksgiving. That which I have vowed I will pay. Salvation is from the Lord" (Jonah 2:9).

V.   Background Reading:
    2 Kings 14–20
    2 Chronicles 26–32

The short Book of Jonah relates an account with which the most unlearned of Bible students are familiar. Jonah's story is one that is filled with suspense, colored with humor and laced throughout with significance. The book has been called, "the most beautiful story ever written in so small a compass," and, in the words of another, "the highwater mark of the Old Testament revelation." Cyprian, an outstanding Christian orator of the third century, was converted through reading this book. So entrenched with respect in the Jewish mind, the book is read on the annual Day of Atonement (Yom Kippur).

The tiny Book of Jonah, too, is probably the most maligned, criticized and ridiculed of all the prophetical books. Nearly 50 years ago in his commentary on the Book of Jonah, Dr. Hart-Davies said: "Jonah is the worst treated book in the Bible. It is the butt of the scoffer: a ready missile which the infidel rarely fails to hurl at the head of the believer; among many professing Christians it serves only to point an inane joke or to provide an inapt smile. Meanwhile the book remains unread, its contents unknown, the preciousness of its revelation undiscovered and unsuspected."

The Nature of the Book

Jonah is not a prophetic book in the sense that it is a collection of prophetic statements (only one sentence, 3:4, can be called prophetic) but rather a biographical narrative. Much of the book's history, however, is predictive or typical. Jonah's stay in the belly of the "great fish" that swallowed him is a picture of the three days and nights our Lord spent in the garden tomb (see Matt. 12:39-41; Luke 11:29-32). Jonah's experience, like those of other biblical personages, are of great value to the servant of Christ who longs for examples to emulate (1 Cor. 10:6, 11).

The parallels of Jonah's experience to the history of Israel are remarkable. Jonah was called to a world mission, to preach God's message to the sinful inhabitants of Nineveh. Israel was called to a similar mission. Jonah initially failed to serve God as he was called, and so did Israel. Jonah's punishment was not unlike Israel who was dispersed among the Gentiles yet remarkably preserved. Upon his repentance, Jonah was recommissioned just as Israel shall be during the Great Tribulation and then will prove to be a source of blessing to many.

As to the book's authenticity, there should be no question. Nothing in the text would indicate that the book is fictional. Both Philo, the famous Jewish philosopher of the first century, and Josephus, the famous historian, refer to the events of the Book of Jonah as historical. The Old Testament historical Book of Kings (2 Kings 14:25) verifies that Jonah indeed prophesied during the days of Jeroboam II, king of Israel. Christ's own testimony (Matt 12:39; Luke 11:29-32) should forever settle any question as to this book's historicity.

The Lessons of the Book

Great lessons await the student who would delve into the Book of Jonah. His flight to Tarshish illustrates the folly of disobeying God. Jonah proves the validity of the Psalmist's declaration that there is no place to which one can flee to escape the presence of God (Ps. 139:7-12). Equally important is the dimension this book provides to our understanding of the mercy of God. Mercy is the loving characteristic of God which causes Him to withhold from us that which we deserve and we see it here experienced by Jonah and the repentent inhabitants of the great gentile city of Nineveh. The phrase "Salvation is of the Lord" (2:9) is the key verse of this significant prophetic book.

The Recipients of God's Mercy

The delicate balance of power in the Middle East was quickly shifting to the Assyrian empire during the reign of Jeroboam II. A prevailing fear occupied the minds of many Israelites that their nation might be consumed by this insatiable giant. Noted for their cruelty, the Assyrians might easily be compared to the worst of German Nazism of a more contemporary area. Assyrian armies skinned their captives alive, pulled out tongues, gouged out eyes and mutilated entire cities by driving over their population with chariots affixed with scythes. They burned boys and girls alive and resorted to other atrocities that were designed to create fear and submission among their subjects. A late British scholar wrote,

> The barbarities which followed the capture of a town would be almost incredible, were they not a subject of boast in the inscriptions which record them. Assurnatsir-pal's cruelties were especially revolting. Pyramids of human heads marked the path of the conqueror; boys and girls were burnt alive or reserved for a worse fate; men were impaled, flayed alive, blinded, or deprived of their hands and feet, of their ears and noses, while the women and children were carried into slavery, the captured city plundered and reduced to ashes, and the trees in its neighborhood cut down.

The capital city of the Assyrian empire was Nineveh, a formidable fortress built on the east bank of the Tigris River. The city had originally been built by Nimrod (Gen. 10:11) and now, at its zenith, was enclosed by a wall over 100 feet high with room at the top for 3 chariots to ride abreast, 1,500 towers rose an additional 100 feet above the wall. Nineveh proper encompassed an area of 350 square miles (20 miles larger than present day London) and boasted a population of over 120,000 (4:11).

It was to this great city and savage people that Jonah was called: "Arise, go to Nineveh the great city, and cry against it, for their wickedness has come up before Me" (1:2 NASB). It was Jonah's initial refusal to go that creates the background for the events recorded in the Book of Jonah.

Why Did Jonah Flee?

The fact that Jonah was commissioned of the Lord to go to Nineveh is somewhat remarkable. Other prophets had denounced wicked cities but had remained in their own country to deliver the message. Jonah was told to make the arduous 500-mile journey across the desert to take God's message of prophetic judgment against the city. The big question is: "Why did Jonah flee?" A review of several of the proposed solutions have been summarized here:

He was afraid to go. It is commonly assumed that Jonah was cowardly—afraid to go to the Assyrian capital. The strength of such an argument loses credence, however, for Jonah exhibits utter fearlessness of death when he pleads with the Phoenician sailors to cast him overboard in the midst of the great storm.

He was a bigot. Some have concluded that Jonah's rationale for fleeing to Tarshish lies in an innate prejudice against the Gentiles. The nationalistic spirit of this prophet is not in question. Jonah *was* a true patriot. His great display of compassion toward the idolatrous gentile sailors, even to the point that he was willing to die for their safety, certainly would argue against bigotry.

He was selfishly jealous. Jonah had established himself a professional reputation in the court of Jeroboam as being an honest and accurate prophet. Perhaps his flight was an effort to maintain this credibility which would undoubtedly be questioned if he prophesied Nineveh's fall only to see the nation repent and the destruction averted. J. Sidlow Baxter observes in his monumental *Explore the Book,* that "it is hard to believe that the prophet who was willing to sacrifice not only his reputation but his life itself for the distressed mariners, would peevishly set his own prestige against all the thousands of lives in great Nineveh."

He knew God was merciful. The answer to the question of why Jonah fled, hazarding the sea which the Hebrews usually avoided, is to be found in the sequel of the story. Jonah states, ". . . for I knew that Thou art a gracious and compassionate God, slow to anger and abundant in lovingkindness, and one who relents concerning calamity" (4:2 NASB).

Jonah was well aware of the suffering inflicted by the Assyrians on other nations and realized that it was only a question of time until Israel would be afflicted in a similar fashion. Frank Gaebelein observed that "Jonah had only to look at the international situation in his day to see the menace of Assyria. Already this great empire had begun to attack Palestine and claim sovereignty over it. . . ." Jonah knew what kind of God Jehovah is and the very fact that God was sending a warning indicated the possibility of repentance and mercy. The prophet had adequately deduced that if Nineveh did not repent she would be destroyed by God. If Jonah refused to go they would not hear nor could they heed the divine opportunity to repent.

Jonah was in a quandary, between the proverbial rock and a hard place! Assyria's salvation would jeopardize Israel's security. Their future and possibly that of his own nation lay in the balance of his decision. However rational his analysis, Jonah was directly disobedient to the command of God. Baxter seems to sum up the need of Jonah best when he writes, "What Jonah needed, and what we all need, if we are to be the Lord's true servants and messengers, is so to get our minds and feelings in the great wide flow of the divine compassions for sinning, suffering, struggling, sorrowing men and women that all lesser considerations are submerged. God's Jonahs must go to Nineveh!"

Jonah's Flight

Jonah's determination to avoid his divine commission brought him to the coastal regions of the Mediterranean where he found a ship in Joppa making preparation to travel to Tarshish, probably identifiable with Tartarus in southwestern Spain. Jonah paid the fare and boarded the vessel. Maybe God might use a substitute messenger for this distasteful task to which he had been called. Perhaps 2,000 more miles away from Nineveh would make him reasonably inaccessible.

The Phoenician ship had not traveled far, however, upon

its journey before trouble arose. The Scriptural record states that "Jehovah hurled a great wind upon the sea" and that which resulted was a storm of such intensity that even those experienced sailors on board feared for their lives. Everyone was quick to recognize that this was no ordinary storm.

After pleading with their gods without avail, the crew resorted to the casting of lots—a common practice in Old Testament times—to determine the culprit who had aroused the anger of the gods. The lot fell on Jonah and upon being exposed the wayward prophet admitted to his guilt in attempting to flee the presence of Jehovah.

The troubled crew queried the prophet as to what action they should take in the light of his admitted guilt. Jonah responded with a promise that the waters would calm once they cast him into the sea. Later attempts to control the tossing ship were ineffective and finally the reluctant sailors adopted the course proposed by the prophet.

The Great Fish

With the casting of Jonah into the sea, the storm subsided and tranquillity was restored. The sailors were astonished at what was clearly supernatural intervention and responded with praise to the God of Jonah (1:16).

The record of what follows has been the subject of ridicule, even among those who are professing Christians. God's preparation of a "great fish" to swallow Jonah (1:17) is remarkable and the subsequent preservation of the wayward prophet is nothing short of miraculous. To reduce the account as mythological is irresponsible and invalidates a commitment to an inerrant revelation while at the same time questioning the very credibility of our Lord who obviously believed the biblical record (Matt. 12:39; Luke 11:29-32). The attempt of some to deny the miraculous caused Frederick Tatford to write: "If God's ways are to be restricted to the limits of finite understanding, we are in serious danger of creating a God who is not much more than Superman. Jonah's story gives an entirely different conception of the Almighty."

It is common to hear references to Jonah and the whale, but it is nowhere stated in the Bible that Jonah was swallowed by a whale. The Book of Jonah makes reference to a "great fish" (1:17) and Christ describes it as a *ketos* (sea monster) in Matthew 12:40. Whether it be a whale (which is a mammal) or another great sea creature, Jonah *was* swallowed and deposited three days later on the eastern shores of the Mediterranean Sea.

A great deal of argument has risen as to the possibility of such an event taking place. While the validity of the account does not rise or fall on the feasibility of the record, it is nonetheless intriguing to note some of the documented accounts of similar instances. In the August 8, 1968, devotional occuring in *The Upper Room* it was written:

> Some people say there isn't a creature in the sea that is capable of performing such a feat. Scientists know better. For instance, in 1912 Captain Charles Thompson harpooned a huge mammal off the coast of Florida which, when it was brought to land, was found to contain another 1,500 pound fish that had been devoured whole. Those who examined Thompson's catch said it could have swallowed 20 average size men! A Baptist minister who came upon the scene stood in the creature's mouth—holding his hands above his head—and still found he was too short to reach the top of the fish's palate.

More striking yet is the incident related by Sir Francis Fox and "carefully investigated by two scientists." The account is as follows:

> In February 1891, the whale-ship *Star of the East* was in the vicinity of the Falkland Islands, and the lookout sighted a large sperm whale three miles away. Two boats were lowered, and in a short time one of the harpooners was enabled to spear the fish. The second boat attacked the whale, but was upset by a lash of its tail, and the men thrown into the seas, one being drowned, and another, James Bartley, having disappeared, could not be found. The whale was killed, and in a few hours the great body was lying by the ship's side, and the crew busy with the axes and spades removing the blubber. They worked all day and part of the

night. Next day they attached some tackle to the stomach, which was hoisted on deck. The sailors were startled by spasmodic signs of life, and inside was found the missing sailor, doubled up and unconscious. He was laid on the deck and treated to a bath of sea-water which soon revived him; but his mind was not clear, and he was placed in the captain's quarters, where he remained two weeks a raving lunatic. He was kindly and carefully treated by the captain, and by the officers of the ship, and gradually gained possession of his senses. At the end of the third week he had entirely recovered from his shock, and resumed his duties.

During his sojourn in the whale's stomach Bartley's skin, where exposed to the action of the gastric juice, underwent a striking change. His face, neck, and hands were bleached to a deadly whiteness, and took on the appearance of parchment. Bartley affirms that he would probably have lived inside his house of flesh until he starved, for he lost his senses through fright and not from lack of air.

The Prayer of Jonah

The second chapter of Jonah records the prayer of the prophet who had experienced a notable deliverance from the wild sea. T. T. Perowne writes:

> The prayer is remarkable for its many resemblances in thought and expression to passages in the Book of Psalms. The words of the Psalter, however, are not exactly and literally quoted, but its ideas and phrases are freely wrought into the prayer, as if drawn from the well-stored memory of a pious Israelite, familiar with its contents and naturally giving vent to his feelings in the cherished forms, which were now instinct for him with new life and meaning.

Many believers can relate similar instances when we have found portions of God's Word that may have been committed to memory years before a "very present help" in our time of trial.

There are two noteworthy aspects of Jonah's prayer worthy of our review:

It is a prayer of thanksgiving. Edward J. Young has correctly observed that "this is not a psalm of thanksgiving for deliverance from a whale's belly. It is rather a song of thanksgiving for deliverance from drowning. The figures of speech employed in this psalm have reference to drowning, not to a whale's belly." This is not a cry for deliverance, for Jonah knew he *was being* delivered! Jonah rejoices in the salvation provided him when he faced certain death having been "cast into the deep, into the heart of the seas" (2:3 NASB).

The prayer does not include petition. This prayer of Jonah is an extraordinary doxology uttered from within the belly of the great fish! It consists of thanksgiving (2:2-6), contrition (2:7-8) and a renewed commitment to Jehovah (2:9). Despite the peculiar location, Jonah realized anew the wonderful love and care of God.

The chapter ends with Jonah being discharged from the whale, safe and sound, in some unknown port of call. From this point the prophet commences his journey to the Assyrian capital of Nineveh.

Jonah's Preaching and Nineveh's Repentance

The mercy of God is beyond human comprehension. Despite man's waywardness, selfishness and disregard of His claims, God condescends to demonstrate His love and compassion and His infinite patience and tenderness to those who so grossly abuse His favor. Jonah came to an appreciation of this mercy in an experiential way and was about to observe that this divine mercy was broad enough to bring forgiveness even to the savage Assyrians.

"Now the word of the Lord came to Jonah the second time, saying, Arise, go to Nineveh the great city and proclaim to it the proclamation which I am about to tell you" (3:1-2). It was to the delivered Jonah that the word of the Lord came this second time. God was prepared to use Jonah again! Of Jonah's readiness, Tatford writes: "Many a sermon has been preached on the vessel which Jeremiah saw marred in the hand of the potter and particularly on the potter's action, *'so he made it again another vessel'* (Jer. 18:4). It was not re-

jected as useless for the master's hand refashioned the clay and produced *'another vessel.'* "

"So Jonah arose and went to Nineveh, according to the Word of the Lord" (3:3). The mission to which Jonah was called was a hazardous one. It was not commonplace for an Israelite to be walking through the city streets of Nineveh! Jonah willingly submitted to the rigors of such an arduous journey and obediently proclaimed the message God had for the city. Apparently the prophet made his way through the city, preaching on the corners the simple message, "... *Yet forty days and Nineveh shall be overthrown"* (3:4).

The spontaneous response to Jonah's message is astounding. "The austere figure of the travel-worn Hebrew prophet with his homely attire," says one writer, "like a stark breath of desert aridity in the midst of the pomp and luxury of pagan Nineveh, caused an unusual reaction which swept like wildfire across the city." The initial curiosity changed to consternation as they began to comprehend the impact of his divine message.

Two things may have contributed to the repentant response of Nineveh recorded in Jonah 3:5-6:

Previous Catastrophes. It is possible that God may have used Jonah as a fourth and final warning to Nineveh. Gaebelein reported that a serious plague swept through the city in 765 B.C. This was followed by a total eclipse of the sun on June 15, 763 B.C. Another plague overcame the inhabitants of Nineveh in 759 B.C. Such events were viewed as very meaningful to ancient people. It *is* possible that God may have prepared Nineveh for Jonah through these prior events.

Jonah was a Sign. Jesus stated that *"Jonah was a sign to the Ninevites"* (Luke 11:30) and it seems that He was referring to the experiences of the prophet. It is likely that Jonah's physical appearance had been changed as a result of his stay in the belly of the fish. Imagine seeing this man, bleached by the gastric juices that had undoubtedly affected him, proclaiming God's judgment upon this wicked people. He was a "sign" to them, a living testimony of the power and influence of God.

The immediate situation accompanied with Jonah's boldness brought great results! A later preacher in Andrew Jackson's day was similarly bold when he allegedly said: "President Andrew Jackson is in the audience today. If Andrew Jackson doesn't repent he will go to hell as surely as any other sinner!" Here was one, like Jonah, that was not awestruck by power but discernably realized that position and influence have their sources in the eternal will of a sovereign and gracious God.

The repentance reported of the Ninevites and led by their king was unquestionably genuine (3:5-9). This was no time for a false penitence. The humbled king issued a proclamation throughout the city, commanding outward signs of penitence and of submission to God. Even the animals (3:7) were to be covered with sackcloth.

Prayer, confession and outward humiliation would be entirely inadequate by themselves. The king made it clear that there must be an accompanying moral reformation. He commanded the citizens of the city to honestly and sincerely turn from their evil way and particularly from the violence which was their national sin.

"When God saw their deeds, that they turned from their wicked way, then God relented concerning the calamity which He had declared He would bring upon them. And He did not do it" (3:10). There had clearly been a change of heart and of conduct; practical living corresponded with the confession that had been made. The people of Nineveh had acknowledged their guilt and had sought the forgiveness of God. Logically, upon their repentance, He graciously and mercifully withheld His proposed action. It was not until over 100 years later that Nineveh met its destiny; this repentant generation was spared the wrath of a Holy God.

The Response of the Prophet

The final chapter of this prophecy is especially significant, for it records a dialogue between Jonah and the Lord. A whole city had turned to God and been delivered from destruction. Instead of rejoicing at the mercy of God and the tremendous response to Jonah's preaching, Jonah was infuriated. He was "displeased" and "angry" for what God had done and asked that his own life be taken (4:3).

The pathetic, sulking Jonah went to the east side of the city as if determined to "wait out" God! The sweltering heat quickly withered the shelter of leaves Jonah had constructed. The Lord, however, graciously "prepared a gourd . . . ."

The "gourd" is generally considered to have been a castor oil plant (*ricinus communis*) or palmcrist. These plants grow profusely in the Tigris Valley, growing to heights of eight to ten feet. While they do grow rapidly, the growth of this plant was miraculously accelerated. The gourd made Jonah exceedingly glad (4:6)!

Jonah's joy was short-lived. The next morning the protective gourd began to wither because a worm that the Lord had prepared had successfully eaten through the stem (4:7-8). This was symbolism Jonah should readily understand. Still Jonah remains steadfast in his position, pitying the lost gourd and again bemoaning his fate.

God posed a critical question to the prophet. The exclusiveness of Jonah was condemned and God made it perfectly clear that He was no tribal deity, restricted to the borders of Israel, but Lord of all (4:10-11). Jonah had pity on a mere gourd, was it not reasonable for the Lord to show compassion in sparing a repentant city of over 120,000? They were the creatures of His handiwork just as Israel and His mercy extended to those whose repentance had resulted in true reformation. Jonah needed to be reminded that the God who knows when a sparrow falls (Matt. 6:26) also exhibits His tender mercies upon all His works (Ps. 145:9).

The Message of Jonah

Everyone can benefit from the message of Jonah. For those who have felt the call of the Lord upon their lives there is the warning not to refuse that call. The book brings comfort to backsliders reminding them that God can still use them. Sinners are shown that true salvation is of the Lord (2:9). The young need to remember to heed God's call (and He has called us all to be available). The old should take comfort that it is never too late to serve the Lord, even in the face of imminent death.

6

Micah: The King
is Coming

KEYS THAT UNLOCK MICAH

I. The Time of the Book: Micah was a Pre-Exilic Prophet to Judah.

II. The Contemporaries of the Prophet: Isaiah, Hosea.

III. The Theme of the Book: God's Judgment.

IV. The Key Verse of the Book: "And He will judge between many peoples and render decisions for mighty, distant nations. Then they will hammer their swords into plowshares and their spears into pruning hooks; nation will not lift up sword against nation, and never again will they train for war." (4:3)

V. Background Reading:
  2 Kings 15:32—19:37
  2 Chronicles 27:1—32:23

The eighth century B.C. was a period of great material prosperity for both Israel and Judah. The military success of Jeroboam II in Israel had enlarged that nation's frontiers. Uzziah, in Judah, had developed the commercial activities of Judah to such a degree that the country was more prosperous than it had been in centuries. A sense of security prevailed in the land. There was peace and no fear of an invader.

The reign of Uzziah in Judah was followed by Jotham, a good king who followed the principles and practices of his father. Jotham, however, was succeeded by the corrupt Ahaz who administered corruption for nearly 20 years. This contemptuous monarch was instrumental in introducing the worship of Baal to Judah, making arbitrary changes in the temple and sacrificing children to Molech. His unscrupulous behavior would leave an irreparable scar upon the history of the nation. Hezekiah, the godly king who succeeded Ahaz, was responsible for initiating considerable religious reforms, changes which appeared to have precious little effect upon the majority of the Judean population. Something sad had happened to men. People practiced worship formally, but there was little room for practicing righteousness in their lives. Reformation was not accompanied by true repentance and few rendered sincere worship to Jehovah. To quote one writer, "Morals were low, government was decadent, courts were corrupt, religion was formalistic, and the nation had lost its integrity."

The first verse of Micah specifically states that the ministry of this native son of Moresheth took place during the reigns of Jotham, Ahaz and Hezekiah. It would seem that this contemporary of Hosea, Amos and Isaiah faithfully contended for God in Judah for over six decades. As to the effectiveness of his utterances, Pusey goes so far as to suggest that the conversion of Hezekiah and many in Judah was probably the final harvest of Micah's life. Whatever the case, this small town prophet left his mark on the nations of Israel and Judah and brought hope to all men by announcing that Messiah would come one day to Bethlehem of Judah (5:2).

The Style of the Book

This prophecy contains several of the prophetic announcements made by Micah during his long ministry. "The book," writes Frederick Tatford in *Prophet of Messiah's Advent*, "is unparalleled for the consistent and unflinching severity of its tone but, at the same time, for its vividness and forcefulness." Keil is more specific in referring to Micah's particular linguistic features when he writes in *The Twelve Minor Prophets,* that "His words are never deficient in cleanness and evenness; whilst in abundance of figures, similes (1:9, 16; 2:12-13; 4:9, and so forth), and rhetorical tropes, as well as in specialty, paronomasia, in play upon words (1:10-15), and dialogue (2:7-11; 6:1-8; 7:7-20), his style resembles that of his highly cultivated contemporary, Isaiah." So frequently have these similarities in style between Micah and Isaiah been noted that Micah has sometimes been designated as "Isaiah in shorthand!"

Micah's prophetic message speaks of a judgment that would come (1–3). The prophet promises a future restoration (4–5) and points out the validity of God's case against the nation (6). The book ends with a statement of the prophet's confidence in God's revealed plan and a new promise of national restoration (7).

The Judgment of Samaria and Judah

The home of the prophet Micah was the tiny village of Morasheth, located on one of the terraces of the Shephelah, that range of low hills between the hill country of Judah and the Philistine plain. Micah's village was less than 20 miles from the home of another prophet of the same period, Amos of Tekoah. It is conceivable that the two prophets were acquainted.

In this strategic location it is likely that an observant prophet could see the political trends of his nation develop. One has written, "Micah must have seen pass by his door the frequent embassies which Isaiah tells us went down to Egypt from Hezekiah's court, and seen return those Egyptian subsidies in which a foolish people put their trust instead of their God" (*The Book of the Twelve Prophets* by G. A. Smith).

Despite the temporary changes caused by Hezekiah's reforms, the sin of the people in Judah and Israel was so deeply ingrained that judgment was inevitable. Micah points out that the wound was incurable (1:8-9)! Society was corrupt, the peasantry were oppressed, and judicial fairness was unheard of in the nation. Micah fearlessly denounced the guilty and declared that Jehovah Himself was about to descend into the arena of judgment!

The Inevitable Judgment

Micah's description of the wrath to come is vivid. His bold announcements of judgment commenced at a time when it was neither expected nor considered warranted. This prophet's disarming message caused no small reaction among those who heard.

Several features of these initial chapters deserve special consideration:

Samaria would become a heap of ruins (1:2-8). The city of Samaria was the pride of Israel. This proud capital city was perched high above the surrounding territory and was considered an impregnable fortress. The very thought that it would become a "heap of ruins" seemed absurd.

Micah begins his prophetic announcements by bitterly condemning the practices that characterized the nation. It was because of the nation's idolatry that the punitive hand of God was to fall upon Samaria. This righteous retribution for sin was long overdue and nothing could avert it (1:8-9).

Micah not only verbalized his message, but he also, in a manner sure to gain the attention of his listeners, outwardly mourned the nation so soon to be bereaved. Micah's appearance was common for the mourners of that day and his "nakedness" suggests "the enforced nakedness of . . . people on their way to captivity (Isa. 20:3-4)" as suggested by Cheyne in his book *Micah*.

Judah's judgment would be quick to follow (1:9-16). As Samaria suffered because of the sins of the nation Israel , it is reasonable to assume that Jerusalem was culpable for Judah's sins. Micah prophesies such judgment (1:9) and, through a series of paronomasias (puns) unparalleled in the Bible, he describes the desolation to come. In his book *The Minor Prophets*, Professor F. W. Farrar provides a translation of verses 10-16 that emphasizes these puns. It reads:

In Gath (Tell-town), tell it not; in Akko (Weep-town) weep not! In Beth-le-Aphrah (Dust-town) roll thyself in the dust. Pass by, thou inhabitress of Shaphir Zaanan (March-town) marched not forth. The mourning of Beth-ezel (Neighbor-town) taketh from you its standing place. The inhabitress of Maroth (Bitter-town) is in travail about good, because evil hath come down from Jehovah to the gate of Jerusalem. Bind the chariot to the swift horse, thou inhabitress of Lachish (Horse-town); she was the beginning of sin for the daughter of Aion, for the transgressions of Zion were found in thee. Therefore wilt thou, Oh Zion, give dismissal (farewell presents) to Moresheth-Gath (The Possession of Gath). The houses of Achzib (False-spring) became Achzab (a disappointing brook) to Israel's kings. Yet will I bring the heir (namely, Sargon, king of Assyria) to thee, thou citizen of Mareshah (Heir-town), Unto Adullam (the wild beasts' cave) shall the glory of Israel come! Make thyself bald (Oh, Zion) for the children of thy delight. Enlarge thy baldness as the vulture, for they are gone into captivity with thee.

All sinners would experience the wrath of Jehovah (2:1-13). The social injustices and the indifference of the very wealthy to the plight of the poor in Israel, so bitterly denounced by the prophet Amos, were also evident in Judah. It is observed in G. A. Smith's book, *The Book of the Twelve Prophets*, that:

the enormous increase of money which had been produced by the trade of Uzziah's reign threatened to overwhelm the simple economy under which every family had its croft. As in many other lands and periods, the social problem was the descent of wealthy men, land-hungry, upon the rural districts. They made the poor their debtors, and bought out the present proprietors.

They absorbed into their power numbers of homes, and had at their individual disposal the lives and the happiness of thousands of their fellow country men. . . . Micah pictures the recklessness of those plutocrats—the fatal ease with which their wealth enabled them to dispossess the yeoman of Judah.

Tatford states in his book *Prophet of Messiah's Advent,* that ". . . Micah makes clear, however, the wrongs of his day went even farther and included judicial corruption, subordination and perversion of justice. More than once in history, these have appeared as the conomitants of social injustice, and have inevitably met with the same divine intervention."

Such behavior could not go by unnoticed and in a series of denunciations Micah presses his case and pronounces wrath upon the land-grabbers (2:1-5) and those who sought to keep him quiet (2:6-7). Their evil deeds would no longer be tolerated (2:9-10). The spiritual discernment of the people was so utterly lacking that they would be quick to accept the message of the false prophet who would, despite their sin, promise blessings of every kind (2:11). Their spiritual sensitivity had evaporated!

God's judgment would fall on the leaders of the nation (3:1-12). The final thrust of Micah's message of "doom and gloom" was directed to the leaders of the nation. It was their responsibility to know the law of God (Exod. 18:25, 16) and people were entitled to turn to them. Instead of shepherding, these ruthless leaders are described as cannibals who figuratively pulled the skin off the people and tore their flesh from their bones to consume it themselves! Because of their evil deeds there was nothing but the unmitigated wrath of a totally just God to be meted out upon them.

Micah's denunciation upon leadership was leveled against the rules of the nation (3:1-4), the false prophets who prevailed in the land (3:5-8) and all other leaders (3:9-12).

Micah's message met with very little positive response. So irritating and upsetting were his threats that a move was quickly made to silence his mournful denunciations. Such efforts did not deter this faithful servant! He continued to speak with conviction the message of Jehovah.

One must not overlook the brilliant promise to the faithful remnant found in the closing verses (12-13) of chapter 2. These comforting words are a solace to the godly and a consistent testimony to the care of God for the righteous.

The Future Restoration

With the prediction of the total destruction of Jerusalem that concluded the previous chapters, it might be deduced that there was no future for the people or the land. The promises of God to Israel were irrevocable and not even the awful sins of the nation could annul those unconditional provisions. In this middle section of the book, Micah proceeds to turn from judgment to painting a picture of the blessings of a future day. The prophet speaks of a kingdom that would be restored (4:1-13) and the coming of a righteous king (5:1-15).

The Restored Kingdom

Micah 3:12 prophesies a destruction so complete that an area once bustling with activity would become a heap of ruins, overgrown with foliage to such an extent that it appears as a forest! In the latter days, however, this situation will be reversed and God will again establish His presence in the land (4:1). Among the features of this restored kingdom are the following:

Zion will be exalted (4:1-2). God will exalt His Holy Mount and the nations will flock to it because the presence of God will be there. Jehovah will be known on the earth and the nations will seek the knowledge of Him.

There will be world peace (4:3-7). The picture of life in this restored kingdom is described in these verses as one of peace and serenity. The righteous king will judge His people and the nations will gladly submit to His leadership. War will be superfluous as He will eliminate such conflict by His just arbitration.

In this serene setting the maimed, afflicted and dispersed

of Israel will be lovingly regathered to take their place forever in this restored kingdom.

Israel will be reunited (4:8-9). The prophet triumphantly announces that the "kingdom would come to the daughter of Jerusalem," a clear reference to a day when Israel and Judah would again be united and Jerusalem would serve as the capital of all the nations. Micah's announcement was obviously of a *literal* kingdom over which God would rule and not some spiritual fantasy. The future of Israel is certain!

All enemies will be defeated (4:11-13). At this time God would sovereignly arrange for the nations of the world who had profaned Israel to be gathered together. These heathen nations gather to gloat over the suffering of God's people, but God's intention was to unite them for judgment. The prophet foresaw the day when divine power would enable Israel to destroy all her foes and stand triumphant as the chosen of God.

The brief glimpse of sunlight shown by Micah is now overshadowed (5:14) by the realities of the present. The judge of Israel, a reference to the king, was about to be humiliated, a probable reference to the imminence of the Assyrian invasion facing the nation of Israel.

The Coming Righteous King

Micah proceeds in turning from the ruler of Israel who had been so grossly insulted by the besieger (5:1) to a monarch of an entirely different order. The coming and life of this coming ruler, the Messiah, is depicted with great clarity in the heart of Micah's prophecy. The special features to be especially noted include the following:

The king's place of birth (5:2). Micah utters one of the most remarkable predictions of his ministry when stating that Bethlehem-Ephratah would be the precise location for the birth of Israel's coming king. By adding the designation "Ephratah," Micah excludes another city of Bethlehem included in the inheritance of Zebulum (Joshua 19:15) and makes reference to a smaller village known as Ephratah (Gen.

35:16, 19; 48:7). This was the home of David (1 Sam. 17:12) and certain of his ancestors (Ruth 1:1-2). It was totally insignificant as a village (a fact borne by its omission from the list of cities initially allocated to Judah in Joshua 15:21-23), but out from among the thousands of Judah it would become paramount due to its being chosen for the site of Messiah's birth.

Something of the unique character of this one to be born in Bethlehem is alluded to in the words which follow: "His goings forth have been from the beginning . . . ." These words, according to Keil in his book *The Twelve Minor Prophets,* "affirms the origin of the Messiah before all the worlds." He was one whose existence stretched back into eternity! This was no new personality that came into existence in Bethlehem's manger. This was the eternal God becoming incarnate.

The king's patience (5:3). Judah suffered under the oppression inflicted by the heathen because of her own infidelity and apostasy. Micah prophesies that the nation's humiliation would be eventually brought to an end at the time of Messiah's birth.

The patience of the Lord with His people stands without question. Stubbornly they have refuted His interventions, yet He has remained faithful. The foes of Israel have attempted to obliterate the nation; yet, true to His infinite faithfulness, God has preserved His people. The coming of the Messiah marks the beginning of Israel's restoration, the complete fulfillment of which awaits a coming day.

The king's person (5:4). The love and care that Messiah would show His people is like that of a shepherd for his sheep. Just as the shepherd, Messiah would watch over His flock, protect them from danger, bind their wounds, satisfy their longings and lead them lovingly into the best pastures.

His rule would be "in the strength of the Lord" (5:4) and that strength would equip Him to perform the work of which He had been called. Those to whom He would minister would abide securely and permanently. Messiah's name will be known among all men as His dominion will extend over the whole earth.

The king's peace and protection (5:5-9). The political situation at the time of Micah created the background for the revelation concerning the peace and protection Messiah would bring to His people. Israel would overcome the current dilemma and a faithful remnant would become as "dew from the Lord" to the nations of the earth. Frederick Tatford speaks to this analogy when writing in *The Prophet of Messiah's Advent*:

> The dew was . . . a night mist resulting from the sudden cooling of the westerly rain-bearing winds by the cold nights which succeed the host eastern days. This mist precipitates its water during the six rainless months and copiously compensates for the lack of rain. Without it the ground would be dried up, plants scorched, and vegetation withered. Through its means, fruits and herbs receive moisture at the critical period and flourish accordingly.

This picture, so vivdly painted by the prophet, was of a restored Israel functioning as a channel of blessing to the nations of the world.

The king's purging (5:10-15). The prophetic forecast continues as the prophet describes the purging that will characterize the entrance of this messianic period. All those things that people had relied upon would be destroyed. War would be waged over all Israel's foes and no amount of military preparedness would protect them from the mighty hand of Jehovah. As Cheyne so aptly relates in his book *Micah*, "Jehovah, being the God of the whole world, is King of the nations (Jere. 10:7); and if the natives have enthroned other gods in His place, and have almost forgotten Jehovah's existence, they are still responsible to Him." No one would escape their accountability to God. Through a spectacular display of divine power the sufficiency of Jehovah would forever be demonstrated to the inhabitants of the earth!

A Plea for Repentance

In his book *The Minor Prophets* F. W. Farrar refers to

chapters 4 and 5 as the "springtide of hope" and chapters 6 and 7 as the "paler autumn of disappointment." This observation of the marked change in tone of the final two chapters of Micah's prophecy is a fitting introduction to the revelation that follows. These concluding chapters focus on the legitimacy of Jehovah's controversy with His people and expresses clearly the spiritual requirements which He longs to see evidenced in the lives of men.

The Legitimacy of God's Complaint

Using the mountains and hills as an independent jury (6:1), the Lord serves as both prosecutor and judge against the nation. The complaint of Jehovah against Israel was based on the following:

The nation had failed to acknowledge the provisions of God (6:3-5). The Lord, by His mighty power, brought Israel out of the land of bondage and waged war with the inhabitants of Canaan. The historical trail of Israel, from Egypt to the Promised Land, testified of the "righteous acts of the Lord." In response to these evidences of divine power, the nation was mute. *They had committed the sin of self-sufficiency.*

The nation sought to atone for her sins through meaningless religious practices (6:6-8). There was no real consciousness of sin in the nation and people engaged in religious practice in a perfunctory manner, seeking in a painless way to discharge their religious responsibilities. As one expositor so pertinently remarked:

> There is not the slightest realization of the unalterable holiness of God, which is satisfied with nothing less than perfect holiness in man (Exod. 19:6; Lev. 11:44, 19:2), perfect love toward God and man (Deut. 6:5; Lev. 19:18; cf. Matt. 22:36-39); no recognition of the wickedness and damnableness of every sin (Deut. 27:26, 28:15-55, 32:22). Nor is there the least desire for mercy, the faintest plea for grace and forgiveness. As His holiness is an offense, so His mercy is a stumbling block to them. They will not be poor beggars before God's throne. They are convinced that

they can merit God's good will by their own efforts. They are willing to bargain with God, as if He were a bargainer like themselves. They are ready to buy His favour, as if He were a venal judge who would overlook their failings if only they paid His price.

Israel had committed the sin of religion, the most subtle of Satan's deceptions, designed to soothe the soul while hardening the heart.

The rich of Israel had abused the poor (6:10-13). The social injustices pointed out clearly by Amos and others of the prophets are again condemned. There was fraud to be seen throughout the nation and such pitiless oppression and deliberate robbing would not pass without the inevitable judgment of God (Gal. 6:7). *Israel had lost her sensitivity to both God and men.*

Israel had forsaken God for the gods of the land (6:16). The most heinous sin of all, spiritual idolatry, consumed the people of Israel. Religious syncretism, as it is frequently called, seemed the most expedient path in a pagan society but its end was death. Conformity to the world led to a loss of identity for the nation and resulted in her being forsaken by God. *The sin of conformity* beckons the saint today. It promises the world and all its pleasures only to lead to fruitless passivity.

The leadership of Israel had become totally corrupt (7:2-5). So dreadful had the situation become that Micah boldly announced that "the godly person had perished from the land." Both prince and people were corrupt and the level of morality had slipped to the point that no one could be trusted. Micah declared that "the best of (men) is like a briar, the most upright like a thorn hedge." (7:4).

The family had lost its identity (7:6). The saddest reflection of the prophet, however, relates to the deterioration of the family unit. All authority within the home had vanished and men of the day found that their greatest enemies were those of their own household (7:6). That very relationship that God had intended to reflect His loving kindness to the world had defiantly created chaos. While Jehovah concludes His description of the charge against the nation with this dreadful picture of the family, it is likely that it was in the home where the national travesty referred to here actually began.

The Hope of Men

Micah's prophecy concludes with a final promise to Israel (7:9-20), but not before the judgment of God has been executed and His divine righteousness satisfied. The prophet rests in the certainty that God will inevitably restore the nation (7:7) and reminds those that afflict Israel that their dominion is temporary (7:8).

The key verse of the prophecy is Micah 6:8, ". . . and what does the Lord require of you, But to do justice, to love kindness, and to walk humbly with your God?" In this verse Jehovah expresses His divine intention for all men that they (1) deal justly with their fellow men, (2) that they love mercy beyond justice, and (3) that they walk humbly with God. Such unselfish concern appealed for here and that "personal relationship" demanded for such a humble walk were the "needs of the hour." The hope of man lay in His relationship to both God and man. Is there no less a need today?

7

Nahum: Reaping the Whirlwind

KEYS THAT UNLOCK NAHUM

I. The Time of the Book: Nahum was a Pre-Exilic Prophet from Judah with a special message to Nineveh.

II. The Contemporaries of the Prophet: Zephaniah, Habakkuk and Jeremiah.

III. The Theme of the Book: God's sovereignty over the nations.

IV. The Key Verse of the Book: "All because of the many harlotries of the harlot, the charming one, the mistress of sorceries, who sells nations by her harlotries, and families by her sorceries." (3:4)

V. Background Reading:
2 Kings 21:1-18
2 Chronicles 33:1-20

For over 200 years the biblical world was dominated by the powerful Assyrian nation. At its zenith the empire stretched from Egypt and the Middle East south to the Persian Gulf. The imperial capital of Nineveh was an imposing and strongly fortified city. It was a prosperous commercial center that encompassed an area of 150 square miles on the east bank of the Tigris River. The river ran by the western wall of the city and on the three other sides the city was protected by moats 150 feet wide. At the time of Nahum's writing, the Ninevites felt they were invincible.

The population of Nineveh is difficult to calculate. Jonah 4:11 makes reference to "more than 120,000 persons who do not know the difference between their right and left hands." This number seems inadequate in view of the immensity of the city and has led Baxter and others to conclude that this represented "infants" unable to make sound judgments. If one took the entire complex beyond the city walls (Greater Nineveh) the number of inhabitants multiplies and might well exceed one million. Since Nahum writes several years after Jonah, the number reported in Jonah 4:11 undoubtedly increased.

Nahum is unique in that his prophecy is not directed to Israel or Judah but to a foreign capital, the city of Nineveh. No attention is given to the sins of God's people. The entire book deals with the destruction of Nineveh whose sins had become intolerable to God. This guilty nation should proclaim a message to our world. Dr. A. Kennedy writes: "Assyria in His (God's) hands becomes an object lesson to the empires of the modern world, teaching as an eternal principle ... the absolute necessity ... that righteousness (personal, civic and national) alone 'exalteth a nation.' "

Jonah had preached to this same city years before and through his preaching impending judgment was averted. The reformation that followed was short-lived and now the sins of this people demanded God's righteous judgment. Pusey writes in his book *The Minor Prophets* that Assyria's preeminent crime was their direct antagonism to the Lord. "It is not simply of rebellion against God, or neglect of Him. It is a direct disputing of His sovereignty. . . ."

The Theme of the Book

There are few books in the Bible that contain so vivid an account of the outpouring of God's wrath upon a people than the Book of Nahum. The reader can almost visualize the attack, plundering and grief of a city that once stood proud among the nations. God's fury upon Nineveh was severe and totally deserved. *It is the righteous nature of God's dealings with the Assyrians that is the theme of this prophecy.*

The Revelation of God in Nahum

The opening chapter (1:2-12) of Nahum contains a remarkable review of the character of God. The dominant characteristic is that of His holiness. It was that predominant feature of His nature that Nineveh and the Assyrian nation had repeatedly ignored. Judgment upon the city was based upon violations of God's righteous character. The appropriateness of the sentence upon Assyria is never placed in question. A sovereign God acted totally within the confines of His character. Among the attributes of His character given special attention by the prophet are the following:

He is jealous over those He loves (1:2). The Old Testament contains repeated claims of the unreserved and exclusive devotion God has for His people. There would be no rival tolerated for He was a *jealous* God (Exod. 20:5).

He avenges those who harm His people (1:2). The jealousy of God had been aroused by the great oppression Israel had suffered at the hands of the Assyrians. God's anger was not a restrained outburst of passion, but it was rather the careful and calculated determination of a sovereign determined to demand full payment from those who had repeatedly violated His will.

He is patient (1:3). God had been long-suffering with the inhabitants of Nineveh. The nation had experienced prolonged existence as a result of the opportunity provided them to repent as a result of the preaching of Jonah. Their persistence in sinning demanded His action. He could not allow them to escape the punishment due them.

He possesses incredible power (1:3). In picturesque language, Nahum declares that the Lord will swoop down upon the guilty in the unrestrained power of the whirlwind (cyclone). The power of God is shown to extend beyond nature to armies that follow His bidding. His power is awesome!

He is good (1:7). This same God of fury was one who displayed compassion and protection to those who placed their confidence in Him. The goodness of God in caring for those He knows is comforting in the midst of personal storms. John Calvin wrote: "To know is just the same as not to neglect; or expressed in a positive form, the care of providence of God in the preservation of the faithful."

He is a refuge for the troubled (1:7). There is no more secure place to be than in the protective hands of an omnipotent God. Such refuge is available to all who know God but can be experienced only by personal appropriation (see Matt. 23:37).

He exercises sovereign power over all men and nations (1:12-14). God is in control! Despite the frustrating circumstances that frequently afflict men, God knows and understands. His power is beyond imagination. It can relieve the burdens men bear. The Lord acts . . . He acts righteously, always within the confines of His character.

He is merciful (1:12). In grace, God gives men that which they do not deserve; in mercy He withholds those things we do deserve. God had mercifully withheld judgment upon Nineveh for years but now He was about to justly punish this nation and graciously relieve His people.

Nineveh's Inglorious Past

The city of Nineveh was the seat of Assyrian power. Proudly glistening on the fertile tablelands of the Tigris, the thriving metropolis depicted power, great wealth and seeming invincible strength. Nahum's prophecies probe far deeper, however, than the secure outward appearance of things to the very heart of the complaint between God and the Assyrians. Among the issues elucidated by the prophet, three are especially prominent.

The nation had viciously persecuted conquered peoples (2:11-13). At this particular time in history, lions had become a general menace in the area around the Fertile Crescent. The lion was repeatedly used in Assyrian sculpture to represent the strength and character of the nation. The use of the lion by Nahum was an appropriate metaphor to describe the wicked practices of the Ninevites. Assyrian armies, like lions, were completely merciless in the treatment of conquered peoples. In his commentary on Nahum, Frederick Tatford writes:

> Just as the lion tore the prey in pieces for his cubs and destroyed animals to provide food for his lionesses, so the warriors of Nineveh spoiled other nations to benefit their own people. As the lion filled his caves and dens with torn carcasses and food for his whelps, so Nineveh, in a plundering lust, had heaped up stores of treasures beyond computation.

Another writes that "the opulence of the citizens of Nineveh came from the predatory campaigns of the Assyrian armies."

The biblical record is confirmed by secular sources. In Ashurbanipal's *Annals* the Assyrian king wrote:

> The remnant of the survivors I laid low at the bullock statues, where they had slain Sennacherib, my grandfather, as an offering to his memory. I let dogs, swine, wolves, vultures, the birds of the heavens, and the sweet-water fish devour their cut-off limbs. . . . I opened their treasuries. Everything which the earlier kings of Elam down to the present day had gathered and heaped up, treasures which no other hand had ever touched before me, those I brought out and counted as booty. . . . I took away with me as booty to Assyria the entire furnishing of his palaces, the articles on which they sat, lay, and from which they had eaten, drunk, washed and anointed themselves, their chariots of war, their gala wagons, their carts, horses, mules, with harnesses of gold and silver."

The nation had persisted in this way of life (3:4). Assyria is likened unto a prostitute who willfully used her glamorous appeal to beguile and enslave foreign nations. Mair (*The Book of Nahum*) writes: "The city's magnificence, the splendor of its palaces and temples, its mighty armies, fabulous wealth, imposing art and architecture—all these are attractions which the brazen adulteress employs in luring victims to their destruction."

Immoral practices are frequently used symbolically in the Old Testament to describe the unfaithfulness of the nation of Israel to the Lord. The imagery here, however, describes the political practices of this wicked nation. There is no suggestion of any affinity between Assyria and the Lord.

Like the harlot, Assyria had chosen this way of life. It was a willful act for which God would hold her responsible.

There was an outward attractiveness of Nineveh which hid the inward corruption (3:4). The casual visitor to the city of Nineveh would have been tremendously impressed. Hidden to the eye was the fact that this city and nation were corrupt to the very core. It was a city full of lies. Pusey comments, however, that "the feet, ears and noses, gouging out eyes, lopping off heads, impaling individuals or flaying them alive was about to be avenged by a sovereign God."

Nineveh had disguised her wickedness by flaunting her materialistic gains. She had successfully rationalized away the horrible price it had taken to satisfy her illegitimate appetite. Her excesses were visually prominent to all who would behold. At the time Assyrian society appeared to be the strongest, the foundation had already eroded beyond repair. No longer would God tolerate their terrible ways; righteous retribution could no longer be averted.

The Judgment Upon Nineveh

When Jonah had predicted judgment upon the city of Nineveh, the inhabitants repented and turned to God. No opportunity to repent was afforded them on this occasion. The strength of Assyria at the time of Nahum's prophecy was so imposing that the threat of total destruction seemed completely absurd. This book, however, vividly portrays Nineveh's fall. In his book titled *The Minor Prophets*, Driver speaks of Nahum's message saying, "He [Nahum] depicts in rapid succession the approach of the assailant, the preparations for the attack, the charging of the chariots, the opening of the gates, the flight of the population, the treasures plundered by the captors, the city which had hitherto been the home of fearless and ferocious warriors . . . became deserted and silent." Among the noteworthy references to the nation's doom, six deserve attention.

No amount of preparation could avert it (2:1; 3:14). As the time of the assault upon Nineveh drew near, the prophet taunted the inhabitants to make extensive preparations for warfare. They had boasted of their invincibility, now was the opportunity to prove themselves! The forthcoming attack would demand personal preparation as well as tactical preparedness (3:14, 25). The more elaborate the preparations for battle the more incredible would be the fall! Nahum's challenges bear a striking resemblance to a prior time when God proved Himself before the godless during the days of the prophet Elijah (1 Kings 18:20-36).

It would be a stunning military conquest (2:3, 3:14). The assault upon the city is prophetically described in the message Nahum delivered. The chariots can be seen tearing through the city streets, their shining metal glistening in the bright sunlight. The very attire of the invaders is announced as being scarlet. The victory over Nineveh was to be complete; not only would multitudes die but the very city would be reduced to ashes. Tatford confirms that,

> Modern excavations confirm that Nineveh was, in fact, destroyed by fire. Charred wood, pulverized stone, statuary baked by the heat, all testify to the truth of the biblical predictions. Secular history also confirms that large numbers of Ninevites actually perished in the fighting. The inspired words were literally fulfilled—and probably in the lifetime of some of those who heard the words when they were first uttered.

There would be consternation among the people of Nineveh (2:5-6). The people of Nineveh were ill-prepared for battle. While their city was constructed with the possibility of attack in mind it seems unlikely that many really expected to defend it against a host of barbaric invaders. At the height of the battle the defenders of the city would be found rushing about in panic, stumbling over one another, in their efforts to save themselves. Nahum paints a picture of panic; of a people who became terrified when their "indestructible" city began to crumble and all of those things which they had spent their lives to accumulate gradually began to erode away.

The end would be unusual (2:6; 3:13). The waters which surrounded the city walls that were intended to be its primary defense proved to be the weapon God used to destroy the city of Nineveh. Nahum prophesied that the river gates would open and that the palace would dissolve (2:6). While some (for example, Feinberg) see this as a picture of the invading army "flooding the city," it seems more logical to conclude that the waters of the bordering Tigris actually did overflow the brick and earth walls reducing them to mud. Kelly (*Lectures in the Minor Prophets*) adopts this position when writing: "It was the waters of the river which dissolved the palatial dwellings and defenses ... the Tigris burst its bounds and swamped and otherwise destroyed a vast portion of Nineveh; so that the very foundations, and not the walls only, were swept away."

The destruction would be complete (2:13; 3:15). Details of the seige upon the city by the combined forces of the Babylonians and the Medes are announced by the prophet from Elkosh. The fate that the Assyrians had pronounced upon so many foes was about to fall upon them. Mair summarizes this best when he writes:

Nineveh is made to suffer the agony, disgrace and destruction she has inflicted on others. She has taken kings captive; now her own royalty will be led away (2:8). She has besieged a hundred enemy cities; now she will suffer siege (3:14). She has spoiled others; now she is to be spoiled (2:10). She has massacred masses of foes; now the multitude of her own slain is staggering (3:3). Her troops have desecrated the temples of vanquished peoples; now her own sanctuaries will be violated. She has set fire to almost uncounted cities; now the flames are to devour her own palaces and homes (3:15). She had ruined cities by flooding water; now she is to be inundated (2:7). Her troops have left conquered cities in ruin; now "desolation and devastation and dilapidation" are to overtake her (2:11). Ruthlessly has she scattered people in exile; now she is to be dispersed beyond regathering (3:16-18). She exhibited captains as a spectacle to her people; now she herself is to be a gazingstock (3:6). She made others flee for their lives; now her own leaders must seek safety in flight (3:17). Nineveh has boasted that she has forever destroyed her opponents' capitals; now an "utter end" is to be made of her 1:8).

The world will rejoice at the fall of Nineveh (3:19). When word was received of the fall of mighty Nineveh, Nahum prophesied that there would be tumultuous rejoicing. The wickedness of the city had been awesome and now restitution on the part of a righteous and sovereign God has been realized!

At the time Nahum prophesied, Assyria was at the height of its prosperity. The possibility of such a severe calamity taking place seemed preposterous. The inspired message was fulfilled to the last detail in 612 B.C. when the city succumbed to the invasion of hostile armies.

Conclusion

Nahum's remarkable prophecy not only related to us the destiny of wicked Nineveh; it also contains a message to the worlds of today. Injustice cannot permanently flourish without ultimately being challenged by the God of the universe. Keil pertinently observed:

> If Nahum's prophecy was thus fulfilled in the destruction of Nineveh, even to the disappearance of every trace of its existence, we must not restrict it to this one historical event, but must bear in mind that, as the prophet simply saw in Nineveh the represen-

tative for the time of the power of the world in its hostility to God, so the destruction predicted to Nineveh applied to all the kingdoms of the world which have risen up against God since the destruction of Asshur, and which will continue to do so to the end of the world.

8

Habakkuk: The Just Shall Live by Faith

KEYS THAT UNLOCK HABAKKUK

I. The Time of the Book: Habakkuk is a Pre-exilic Prophet from Judah.

II. The Contemporaries of the Prophet: Zephaniah, Nahum and Jeremiah.

III. The Theme of the Book: The Just Shall Live by Faith.

IV. The Key Verse of the Book: "Behold, as for the proud one, his soul is not right within him; but the righteous will live by his faith." (2:4)

V. Background Reading:
   2 Kings 23:31—24:7
   2 Chronicles 36:1-8

Habakkuk might well be the most unique book in the Bible. Unlike all the other prophets, Habakkuk addresses his message to God alone and not to Judah, Israel or the nations that geographically surrounded God's people. The other prophets transmitted God's message to the people with exhortations to repent and turn to God; Habakkuk complains to the Lord regarding the apparent inconsistencies of His dealings. This dialogue between the prophet and God focuses on two major questions: (1) Was evil to remain forever unpunished? and (2) How could a holy God use unholy instruments to achieve His ends? God patiently dealt with the indignant prophet and Habakkuk eventually gained a renewed confidence in God's sovereignty. The triumphant conclusion declares that in the depths of adversity the prophet's joy would be forever in Him (3:17-19).

The Dilemma of the Prophet

Habakkuk ministered to the nation Judah in those days immediately prior to the Babylonian captivity. These were dark days in the land. The reformation of Josiah had been forgotten, the monarchy in Judah was corrupt and violence and injustice characterized the attitudes of the general population. Charles Feinberg wrote of the situation, "Ensnaring the righteous by fraud, the ungodly perverted all right and honesty." Jehoiakim reigned as king in Judah. Driver writes of Jehoiakim that he

> was a selfish and tyrannical ruler. At a time when the country was impoverished by the collection of the tribute imposed by Necho, he developed a passion for regal magnificence; as Jeremiah tells us (Jer. 22:13-17), he built by the forced, by unpaid, labour of his subjects a spacious palace "panelled with cedar, and painted with vermilion"; he moreover abused his position to indulge in the common vices of an Oriental despot—his eyes and his heart were set only "upon dishonest gain, and for to shed innocent blood, and for oppression and for violence for to do it." As the allusions in Jeremiah show clearly, the reformation of Josiah had affected the masses only superficially: though there were still faithful

souls left, lawlessness, injustice, dishonesty, and oppression were only too rife in the nation at large, and idolatry was widely and openly practiced (Jer. 11:10; 14:7, 10-12, 20).

It was this situation that prompted the dialogue between the prophet and God which introduces this book. The prophet was perplexed with the silence, inactivity and apparent unconcern of God over these appalling conditions. Habakkuk bares his heart to God (1:2-4) seeking the answers to the question that every generation has asked, "Why do the righteous suffer when the wicked seem to flourish?" Stephens-Hodge writes in the *New Bible Commentary:*

> Such a question could arise only in Israel. Only to men who believe in one God, who is both holy and good and is at the same time the omnipotent creator and upholder of the universe, can there be any real problem of theodicy. The dilemma, "If God, then why evil?" is no dilemma to those who believe in a pantheon of warring deities whose morals are hardly different from those of men and women. The thought of God's undeviating righteousness at once creates a tension in the light of everyday experience and demands an explanation.

And so Habakkuk cries to God. It seemed, though, that the heavens were as brass. Here men suffered under the oppression of the royal household, the poor and innocent were the victims of calculated mischief and God did not act. The godly cried for vengeance, pleading with God to vindicate His own holiness, but nothing. It all seemed so inexplicable. Sir Robert Anderson, in *The Silence of God,* says that it was one of those times

> when, in the language of the old Psalm, "heart and flesh cry out for the living God" (Ps. 84:2). The *living* God: not a mere Providence, but a real Person—a God to help us as our fellow man would help if only he had the power. And at such times men pray who never prayed before; and men who are used to praying, pray with a passionate earnestness they never knew before. But what comes of it? "When I cry and call for help He shutteth out my prayer" (Lam. 3:8): such is the experience of thousands . . . no novel experience with men that heaven should be silent.

Anderson concludes that such absolute and prolonged silence "tries faith and hardens unfaith into open infidelity."

Habakkuk begins with a complaint! The burden had become too great; the questions too perplexing. The prophet *needed* the answers from God!

The Instrument of God

As perplexing as the apparent silence of God in the face of such blatant sin among His chosen people was the astonishment caused by the announcement that judgment would take place at the hand of the Chaldeans (Babylonians). God's plan seemed totally unreasonable to Habakkuk. How could *God* use the wicked Chaldeans as His instrument to judge the comparative godly nation of Judah? Twelve verses (1:5-17) are devoted to describing the nation which would descend upon Judah like a famished beast. Noteworthy are the following observations:

Babylon possessed an unquenchable appetite for world domination (1:5-6). The Babylonians are described by Laetsch in *The Minor Prophets* as follows:

> ... impetuously rushing on, never resting until their goal was reached. The rapidity with which the Chaldean or Neo-Babylonian Empire became the ruling world power is almost unbelievable. Nabopolassar's revolt against Assyria in 626 B.C. was crowned with success. Only 13 years later (612) proud Nineveh lay at his feet a heap of ruins. Seven years later, Egypt, the only remaining rival for world supremacy, was disastrously defeated by Nebuchadnezzar, the crown prince, who pursued Necho and his army as far as Egypt (605). Jerusalem was destroyed in 586, Egypt overrun and humbled in 568. ... In their insatiable hunger for world power, the Chaldeans were not satisfied with acquiring unoccupied areas; they marched through the length and breadth of the land, lusting particularly for the conquest of countries inhabited by other nations.

The Bible's description of their warmongering ways is totally compatible with the historical record. Schlier declares that they were "a people, insolent and eager for conquest." Tatford concurs in his observation in the *Prophet of the Watch-*

tower: "The Chaldean armies swept through the country, ruthlessly liquidating all adversaries, seizing loot and property for themselves, and showing a complete lack of mercy or compassion."

The Babylonians were tyrannical in the treatment of captives. Habakkuk describes them as a "bitter and hasty nation," a reference to their cruelty and the relentless way they treated their fellow man. The merciless barbarities employed by the earlier Assyrians were copied only too fully by the Chaldeans. The specific act of separating a people for the land was practiced extensively. This reduced the threat of resistance among conquered peoples and also enabled the Chaldeans to acquire gifted individuals who might function effectively in Babylonian life.

The Babylonians were indignant toward the rights of men (1:9-10). So confident were the Babylonians in their own strength, they scoffed at kings and mocked insignificant rulers. They arrogantly established their own laws (1:7) and demanded unreserved obedience to them. Their burning desire for potential new conquest dictated their priorities. A man's value was predicated on his ability to assist in reaching their goals.

The Babylonians scorned the power and reality of God (1:11). There was no room for a sovereign God in their theology. They praised their own strength as the cause of their triumphs. Their might was their god! The more successful they became in their military endeavors, the more arrogant they became. "Might is right" was their theme; their power was their real god.

The Answer from the Lord

Habakkuk boldly issued his complaint to the Lord. He was perplexed by the ways of God, unable to comprehend how God could use a ruthless nation like Babylon as the instrument of His judgment. Certain that he would be rebuffed, the prophet climbed like a sentinel to the watchtower where he would await the divine reply.

There is a sense of tenderness that can be seen in this book that could be overlooked in a casual reading. Habakkuk nearly denounces God for His actions and appears almost brash in his demand for an explanation. One gets the impression that the prophet climbs the watchtower ladder to sit almost daring the Lord to defend Himself. The concern of Habakkuk was real and his questions, no matter how impassioned, were a legitimate product of his incomplete understanding of God's ways. The Lord deals tenderly with His servant in revealing His program more fully to him.

Habakkuk 2:1-3 is a prelude to the fuller revelation God provides concerning the demise of the Babylonians. The section is introduced (2:1) by an indication of the prophet's belief that God would honor his inquiry with a suitable explanation. *Even though Habakkuk could not understand why God was acting in the way that He was, he never gave up on God! Never did he doubt the propriety and wisdom of the divine actions.*

Three features of God's announcement in verses 2 and 3 deserve special consideration:

The matter of Babylon was settled with God. God is unlike men who improvise to meet unexpected challenges. Babylon's place in His eternal program was settled. The unrepentant inhabitants of Judah would be punished by God at the hand of these tyrannical invaders, but they too would eventually suffer the righteous wrath of a Holy God. History has recorded the appropriate words of Anne of Austria who told Richelieu, "God does not pay at the end of every day, my Lord Cardinal, but at the end He pays." The Apostle Paul related the same truth to believers in Galatia when he wrote, "Be not deceived, God is not mocked, whatsoever a man soweth, that shall he also reap" (Gal. 6:7). God would take care of Babylon!

Judgment would be according to God's timetable. The prophet was told, "For the vision is yet for the appointed time; it hastens toward the goal, and it will not fail. Though it tarries, wait for it; for it certainly will come, it will not delay" (Hab. 2:3). The judgment God pronounced upon

Babylon was not necessarily imminent. While fixed in the divine mind, its fulfillment might seem slow in coming. Habakkuk was exhorted to patiently wait. Many a committed Christian has waited long to experience the reality of God's promises to him and has learned that He who had declared it to be is faithful to perform it (1 Thess. 5:24). All of us occasionally need to be reminded, as Calkins so aptly states in *The Modern Message of the Minor Prophets,* that "God's train is never late. It will arrive on scheduled time. A time limit is set in the counsels of God to the triumph of evil over good."

The faithfulness of the righteous will always prevail (2:4). The wicked may prosper for a time, but their end in judgment is both inevitable and inescapable. One has written, "When a nation is committed to self-aggrandizement through oppression of others, it has written its own obituary." Babylon's doom was settled with God and the reward of the faithful righteous is again established. This concluding phrase of verse four, ". . . but the righteous shall live by his faith (or possibly faithfulness)" is quoted three times in the New Testament (Rom. 1:17; Gal. 3:17, and Heb. 10:38). While the context for each reference differs, in each case the quotation commends the faith of men in God as the primary Christian virtue enabling men to not only experience the life freely offered in Christ, but also to sustain and give substance to hope and to demonstrate the reality of the invisible (see Tasker, *The Gospel of the Epistle to the Hebrews,* p. 60). Such faith will always prevail.

The Basis of God's Judgment

The final verses of chapter 2 (vv. 6-20) are a portrayal of the Chaldean way of life and compose a tacit pronouncement of the fate that will accompany such conduct and wicked practices. Frederick Tatford summarizes in the *Prophet of the Watchtower* each of the five "woes" as follows:

(1) Woe against aggression (2:6-8)

(2) Woe against self-assertion (2:9-11)
(3) Woe against violence (2:12-14)
(4) Woe against inhumanity (2:15-17)
(5) Woe against idolatry (2:18-20)

The Chaldeans had plundered many nations and merciless destruction could be evidenced in every country which they had conquered. They had established for themselves a "house" (or dynasty) and elevated themselves from among the nations through robbery and injustice. Frank Gaebelein suggests in his *Four Minor Prophets* that a house "reflects the personality of those who dwell in it." Rudyard Kipling is quoted as saying, "Men and women may sometimes, after great effort, achieve a creditable lie; but the house, which is their temple, cannot say anything save the truth of those who have lived in it." This "house" of the Chaldeans testified only of rapacious plunder and ill-gotten gain. The horrible violence and the inhumanity shown their captives would be visited upon them. Chaldea would reap what she had sown. She would be ruthlessly victimized by those nations she had so brutally maltreated. The spoiler would be spoiled and her "dumb idols" (2:18-20) would silently watch, incapable of intervening.

The Response of the Prophet

The final chapter of this prophecy is described as a prayer (3:1), but it might more appropriately be designated a hymn of praise. The prophet had listened as God revealed His purposes, first in the castigation of Judah and then the retributive judgment upon the Chaldeans. God had shown Habakkuk that His plans were vast and incomprehensible to men. This revelation of God's sovereignty over the creation left the prophet in awe. The circumstances that troubled Habakkuk had not changed, but this concluding ode reveals a dramatic change in His understanding. Troubled as he was, he pours out his soul. Among the noteworthy aspects of this concluding chapter, three things should be especially observed.

The prophet prays for revival (3:2). The judgment to befall Judah was seen by Habakkuk as the inevitable result of the nation's sin. Yet, troubled as he was by this realization, Habakkuk pleads for a fresh manifestation of divine power. By implication he acknowledges the justice of God's action. He prays, though, that even in the outpouring of wrath, God might remember mercy. Some have suggested that this plea is not so much for judgment to be tempered with mercy as it is a petition that the entire process be speeded up.

The Lord reveals Himself at work in the world (3:3-15). Much of this final chapter is devoted to a solemn description of God at work in the world. In the most vivid of terms the prophet is caught up to another sphere where he is shown the outpouring of judgment from another perspective. All the preparations of men to avert the wrath of God are seen as futile. In avenging wrath Jehovah thrashes the nations. Just as the ox tramples the grain on the threshing floor, so God was to trample the nations (Micah 4:13). The picture given the prophet undoubtedly disclosed the purpose of God in regard to the Chaldeans. Habakkuk, however, saw far beyond the immediate to a more distant time when God would intervene on behalf of His people.

The victory of faith (3:16-19). Habakkuk heard the voice of God in the storm and realized that there would be ultimate salvation for Israel. Despite his fear and apprehension in the judgment to come (3:16) there developed an absolute confidence in the power, presence and purposes of God. There is a resolve on behalf of the prophet seen in these closing verses (vv. 17-19) that defies human understanding. He had seen the greatness of God and knew His mighty power; he had been taught that, whatever happened in the present, the future was ultimately assured. C. A. Dinsmore has aptly written in *The English Bible as Literature* that "God does not explain, but He does give to the anguished spirit such a sense of the Divine that questioning ceases in the peace of submission. He does not answer the interrogations of the mind, but does satisfy the profound yearnings of the spirit . . . ." Nothing that man can do can thwart the promises and program of God.

Nothing at all!

9

Zephaniah: Prophet of Royal Blood

KEYS THAT UNLOCK ZEPHANIAH

I. The Time of the Book: Zephaniah was a Pre-Exilic Prophet of Judah.

II. The Contemporaries of the Prophet: Zephaniah ministered during the prophetic ministries of Nahum, Jeremiah and Habakkuk.

III. The Theme of the Book: The Day of the Lord.

IV. The Key Verse of the Book:
"But I will leave among you a humble and lowly people, and they will take refuge in the name of the Lord" (3:12).

V. Background Reading:
2 Kings 22:1-2
2 Chronicles 34:1-7

To all those who feel that their voice is meaningless in a world that is characterized by its disbelief—take heart! For the skeptics who are determined that revival can't take place in this pagan society—beware! There's a challenge awaiting you in the study of the Old Testament prophecy of Zephaniah.

Zephaniah lived in an age like ours, a time when paganism and idolatry were running rampant. True religion had been so polluted that few knew how to truly worship. Materialism had gotten out of control; simple justice had gone "into hiding."

Enter Zephaniah. Zephaniah, the prophet of royal descent (1:1), was a man who had a lot to lose. But in this atmosphere of unbelief he made scathing denunciations and threatened divine judgment more boldly than most of his contemporaries. Boldly he predicted an awesome day in which Jehovah would vent His wrath mercilessly upon the ungodly. That *day* was imminent!

And men repented! An entire nation was given a new lease on life because they turned again to God and His Word. What influence Zephaniah actually had in this change instigated by Josiah's discovery of the law is purely speculative. This writer would like to believe, though, that Josiah's actions were prompted by a realization of the validity of Zephaniah's claims. Whatever the case, this direct descendent of godly King Hezekiah had the courage to stand alone when others resolutely persisted in their apathy and disobedience!

Approaching the Book

Zephaniah's uniqueness among the prophets lies in the comprehensive manner in which he presents the prophetic message. This special aspect was noted in Bucer's commentary of 1528 when he wrote: "If anyone wished all the secret oracles of the prophets to be given in a brief compendium, let him read through this brief Zephaniah." Keil concurred with this evaluation when he wrote in *The Twelve Minor Prophets* that Zephaniah reproduced "in a compendious form the fundamental thoughts of judgment and salvation which are common to all the prophets."

Seven times in this brief prophecy the phrase "the day of the Lord" appears. The prophet continually reminds his readers of the presence of the Lord in their midst (3:5, 12, 15, 17) and appeals for the nation of Judah to repent. As in most of the prophets, Zephaniah concludes with the promise of ultimate blessing (3:16-20) upon the nation Israel.

Zephaniah might be referred to as the "Polaroid Prophet." His prophecy is void of lengthy dissertations characteristic of some of his contemporaries (for example, Jeremiah), but he does accurately provide three successive "snapshots" of life as it existed in Judah at the time of his writing (1:1–2:3), life around the world of his day (2:4–3:8), and life as it would be following the repentance of Israel (3:9-20).

Wrath Coming on Judah

Zephaniah begins his prophetic message by graphically depicting the awful wrath God was about to pour out upon the inhabitants of Judah. This time is referred to as "the day of the Lord" (1:7).

The Day of the Lord refers to any period of time when God sovereignly intervenes in judgment upon any people. The time is frequently used in reference to a future period in which God will ultimately halt the wickedness of men during the Great Tribulation. All references, however, to this day are not necessarily direct prophetic referrals to this future tribulation. Zephaniah and others of the Old Testament prophets would speak of the "day of the Lord" as that time when God would intervene in imminent judgment upon the nations to whom they had been called to minister. The judgment and captivity by Babylon, for instance, seem clearly referred to by Zephaniah to this dreadful day. Any referral to the "day of the Lord" in the prophets, however, is clearly an anticipation or foreshadowing of that final day of God's wrath. This phenomena may be called "the near and far view" of prophecy.

The Picture of the Wrath to Befall Judah

The opening chapter of Zephaniah's prophecy depicts the judgment about to befall the nation of Judah. Two specific aspects of this "day of the Lord" are brought into focus by the prophet: the extent of the judgment and a description of its fulfillment.

The extent of the judgment (1:3-9). The coming of Zephaniah must have shattered the complacency and self-sufficiency of the inhabitants of Judah. No living thing would be exempt from the wrath of God. God's outstretched hand (1:4) symbolized His preparation for punitive action. Every man and woman in the land was to feel the weight of this hand!

Among those upon whom Jehovah's terror was reserved were the Baal worshipers (1:4), the astrologers and idolaters (1:5), apostates, atheists and agnostics (1:6) and the king's sons (1:8). None would escape who had compromised truth for the expediency of unity in a pagan world. Obedience to the revelation of God was the criteria upon which men would be judged! They stood without excuse.

While the prophecy of Zephaniah was written over 25 centuries ago, his message retains its relevance today. The tolerance toward false doctrine and practices so common today among "evangelicals" smacks a very familiar ring to the syncretism of the worship of Jehovah with that of false deities existent in Zephaniah's day. Will the God who has shown amazing grace and mercy and who has withheld the merited punishment for so long always persist in postponing judgment?

The judgment described (1:10-18). Lest there be any question as to the nature of the coming judgment, Zephaniah vividly describes some of the features of the coming "day of the Lord" in these latter verses of chapter 1.

So intent will be the onslaught of plunder that the shrieking of the population would resound through the streets of the city (1:10). Specific locations are alluded to including the Fish Gate and the Second Quarter (1:10). So thorough was the effectiveness of the invasion that a "search of Jerusalem with candles" would not reveal one exempt.

The plea for repentance (2:1-3). Zephaniah concludes this first prophetic "snapshot" by insisting on the logic of repentance in the light of the forthcoming judgment.

"Gather together," the prophet exhorts, "assemble yourselves as a nation while opportunity is still available to delay the execution of God's wrath." Charles Feinberg writes that "the word translated 'gather together' ordinarily means to gather together stubble as fuel for burning . . . the Nation is addressed in a derogatory manner because of their sin." The summons to repent and demonstrate adequate contrition for their sin was Judah's only hope. Only through such action could they hope to have shelter from the storm of God's wrath looming on the horizon.

The Picture of Zephaniah's World

The coming wrath of Jehovah was not restricted to the inhabitants of Judah. The effects would be felt by all the gentile nations. In one all-consuming sweep the prophet pronounces judgment to those nations to the west (2:4-7), then to the east (2:8-11), south (2:12), and north (2:13-15).

Judah's neighbors were ripe for punishment! The very names of the pagan coastal cities testified of their pompous arrogance. Pusey notes how their sentence is pronounced by Jehovah by a slight change in their title.

> Azzah (Gaza), strong shall be Azoobah, desolated; Ekron, deep-rooting, shall be Teaker, uprooted; the Cherethites, cutters off, shall become Cheroth, diggings; Chebel, the land of the sea-coast, shall be in another sense Chebel, an inheritance, divided by line to the remnant of Judah; and Ashdod, the waster, shall be taken in their might, not by craft, nor in the way or robbers, but driven forth violently and openly in the noonday.

Eventually they would be void of the bustle that characterized them in their arrogance and they would become the pasture lands of the nomadic shepherds of the land. The prophecies of Zephaniah were fulfilled to the letter when hordes of Scyntians wiped out the inhabitants of the coast and left their land bare!

To Judah's east were the Moabites and Ammonites (2:8-10) whose descent can be traced to an incestuous relationship between Lot and his daughters (Gen. 19:36-38). These enemies of Judah were notorious for their pride and haughtiness (Isa. 16:6), their idolatry (1 Kings 11:7), and inhumanity (2 Kings 3:27). Their opposition to God's people was not only evidenced in their actions toward them (Jer. 48:1–49:6, Ezek. 25:1-11), but also in their rejoicing when calamity was suffered by Judah.

The justice of God would be satisfied, however, and the picture of the wrath to befall these haughty nations leaves little to the imagination. The land would become desolate (2:9) and the inhabitants of these nations would be deprived of their idols (2:11), left only with the stark reality of God's awesome presence. These haughty nations could not escape the consequences of their actions towards others and had to learn that there is indeed a God in heaven to whom they *must* answer.

The focus of Zephaniah's attention moves from Ammon to Ethiopia in the south (2:12) whose judgment, too, is pronounced by God.

The judgment of Assyria, to the north, concludes the panoramic picture of judgment given by the prophet in this section of the book (2:13-15). The great Assyrian Empire dominated the ancient world from the ninth to the seventh century before Christ. Nahum had prophesied the end of Nineveh, the bloody city (Nahum 3:1), and Zephaniah boldly announces that this once magnificent city would become a complete desolation. Of such a judgment, Pusey writes in his book *The Minor Prophets*:

> No desolation is like that of decayed luxury. It preaches the nothingness of man, the fruitlessness of his toils, the fleetingness

of his hopes and enjoyments, and their baffling when at their height. Grass in a court or on a once beaten road, much more, in a town, speaks of the passing away of what has been. . . . It leaves the feeling of void and forsakenness. But in Nineveh not a few tufts of grass here and there shall be token desolation, it shall be one wild, rank pasture, where flocks shall not only feed, but lie down, as in their fold and continual resting-place, not in the out-skirts only or suburbs, but in the very center of her life and throng and busy activity.

The clear picture is one of tragic destruction! Nineveh, too, could not escape the hand of God's justice.

Jerusalem

Judah's neighbors were well worthy of their predicted judgment. Zephaniah concludes his panorama by pointing out that Jerusalem, the impenitent capital of Judah, was no better than her pagan neighbors. The magnificent city of David had sunk so low that the prophet refuses to address her as the "city of peace," but described her instead as the "city of oppression." Jerusalem, more highly privileged than the gentile nations neighboring her borders, had rejected every means of grace God had bestowed and had obstinately turned her back on Jehovah.

The unchanging, unfailing justice of God (3:5) is the ulti-mate measure by which the fate of all men is determined. Judah had been given vivid examples (3:6-7) which should have served as silent reminders of the divine character. God's chosen nation had been so insensitive in failing to heed the divine voice that they, too, were testing the seeming un-limited mercy of God. Judgment was imminent for Judah, too!

The Picture of Israel's Remarkable Future

The final "snapshot" given by the prophet Zephaniah pic-tures life as it will be during the millennial age. Among the features of Zephaniah's eschatological picture, the following deserve special consideration:

People will have a pure lip (3:9). Whether this refers to a new language (and hence a reversal of the judgment of Babel recorded in Gen. 1:7-9) or a purified heart made evident in cleansed conversation is somewhat debatable. However one views this, it *is* evident that a dramatic change in the basic character of mankind will be readily observable during this period.

Israel will be restored to her land (3:10-13). Zephaniah looks to that time when God would gather out of all nations those of His people whom, centuries before, He had dispersed as a penalty for their unrighteousness. Those who return to the land in this day will be a humble and lowly people, exhibiting none of the wicked characteristics of the past. Their trust and confidence will be solely in Jehovah.

The King of Israel will be in their midst (3:15). Messiah, the promised anointed one, will dwell in the midst of the nation. This cause of praise and jubilation would gain expression in singing as those restored exult the presence of Jehovah with a full heart!

Israel will experience, as never before, the love of God (3:17). Jehovah Himself would now rejoice in His people! In referring to the phrase "silent in His love," Keil writes, in his book of *The Twelve Minor Prophets*, that here is an expression used to denote love so deeply felt that it is silent, absorbed in its object with thankfulness and admiration. Such an expression of pleasure and gladness would characterize life in Israel's glorious future.

10

Haggai: The Prophet that Motivated

KEYS THAT UNLOCK HAGGAI

I. The Time of the Book: Post-Exilic Prophet to Judah.

II. The Contemporaries of the Prophet: Zechariah and Ezra.

III. The Theme of the Book: Rise up and Build!

IV. The Key Verses of the Book:
"Now therefore,... Thus says the Lord of hosts, 'Consider your ways!' " (1:5-7).

V. Background Reading:
Ezra 5:1–6:15

The Old Testament prophecy of Haggai, referred to by J. Sidlow Baxter as "a momentous little fragment," covers a period of only about four months, but it deals with one of the most crucial periods in the history of the nation Israel.

Much of the nation Judah, in fulfillment of a warning given to King Hezekiah years before (Isa. 39:6-7) and because of her continued deplorable sin, was destroyed by King Nebuchadnezzar in 586 B.C. (2 Kings, chapters 24 and 25). The servitude imposed by God upon the nation was determined to be 70 years (Jer. 25:11). The prophecy of Ezekiel and Daniel's writing provide a glimpse of what life was like for the nation during this 70-year period of chastisement.

Upon the humiliating defeat of Babylon in 539 B.C. by the Persians, one of the first actions by the Persian ruler Cyrus was to issue a decree authorizing the exiled Jews to return to their own land. Cyrus' action was extraordinarily announced years before by the prophet Isaiah (Isa. 44:28)! The sacred artifacts stolen by Nebuchadnezzer were returned and the nation was provided with funds to assist in the reconstruction of the temple (2 Chron. 36:22-23; Ezra 1:1-4, 7; 3:7). In 436 B.C. the caravan of initial Jewish exiles (estimated to be about 200,000 men, women and children) began their arduous journey around the fertile crescent to their fallen nation.

The land to which they returned lay desolate. Disfigured by fire and little more than a mass of blackened stone and debris, the cities were overgrown and undoubtedly inhabited by the wandering Bedouin tribes so common to Palestine. After initially searching out the land, rubble was cleared in front of the former temple site so that the altar could be erected (Ezra 3:3). The completion of the altar was cause for great celebration.

Shortly after the altar was completed, the foundation of the second temple was laid causing great rejoicing by some and loud weeping by others who were saddened by contrasting this lowly building project with Solomon's glorious temple (Ezra 3:8-13). From 536-520 B.C. the temple work was halted due to the interference of the pagan neighbors of Judah who had been refused to share in the building reconstruction (Ezra 4:1-5).

At the time Haggai commenced his ministry, 16 years had transpired. Baxter writes, "the temple remained unbuilt, and the foundations were silted with debris and overgrown with weeds. The repatriated nation seemed to have accepted the situation with an almost fatalistic resignation." Enter the prophet!

Haggai, in a series of four messages, arouses the nation to rebuild the house of God. This powerful preacher condemned their ways and boldly urged them to evaluate their priorities in the light of their exalted position as the chosen of God. His success is unquestioned for through his appeals the work commenced!

The Authority of the Book

The exiles from Babylon had been led to Jerusalem by the high priest, Joshua, and by Zerubbabel, who became their civil governor. Joshua (or Jeshua) was in the direct line of high priests, his father being Jozadak (Ezra 3:2), one of those taken captive by Nebuchadnezzar (1 Chron. 6:15). Zerubbabel was the grandson of Jehoiachin and as such was recognized by the Jews as the legitimate heir to the throne. As the Davidic heir, Cyrus appointed him as the governor of this returning remnant. It was to these two men that Haggai's first words were addressed.

A striking feature of the Book of Haggai is its emphasis upon the divine authority of its messages. In 38 verses and less than 2 printed pages, divine authority is claimed no less than 29 times! The expression "the word of Jehovah came" occurs 5 times (1:1, 3; 2:1, 10, 20) and its counterpart "thus saith Jehovah of hosts" is employed by Haggai 4 times (1:2, 5, 7; 2:11). On 19 other occasions the name "Jehovah" is used with the words "saith," "voice," "messenger" or "sent," all clearly designating God as the source of this message.

Haggai's prophetic messages are clearly dated (1:1; 2:1, 10, 20) and are written within four months of each other during Darius' second year (520 B.C.). This would make Haggai a contemporary of both Zechariah and Ezra.

The Outline and Key Phrase

The four messages of the prophet provide a suitable outline for studying the book. In his first message (1:1-15) the prophet seeks to *arouse* the people of Judah to build the temple. The second message (2:1-9) is one of *encouragement* to continue the task. In the third address (2:10-19) the prophet argues from the ritual law to *confirm* the necessity of their labors and a final message (2:20-23) of *assurance* is given to the governor, Zerubbabel.

The key phrase of the book is "consider your ways." This admonition is repeated five times and is an encouragement to the nation to seek the direction of God in establishing personal and national priorities (see Matt. 6:33).

The First Message

The first message of the prophet summoned Zerubbabel and Joshua to rebuild the temple. The nation was accused of regarding their own material comforts above the reconstruction of the temple. Sixteen years of neglect had been observed by God who had punished them through a series of natural calamities in an effort to remind them of their failing to attend to one of the most important concerns of their time. The Lord now sends His prophet to arouse a population out of their lethargy to meet the challenge of the day.

The failure to rebuild the temple was initially attributable to the opposition of the nation's neighbors to the reconstruction project (Ezra 4:1-3). William Kelley in his *Lectures Introductory to the Minor Prophets* notes that "it was not unnatural that the Jews should be afraid of their watchful enemies; but they should have looked to Jehovah. Where there is simplicity of confidence in the Lord, it is astonishing how the tables are turned, and the adversaries stand in dread of the feeblest folk who have faith in the living God." The altar was completed earlier and was, as one writes, "an admirable testimony to their faith," but they allowed it to become a substitute for the temple!

Other reasons for their neglect are not far removed from excuses entertained in our day for failing to follow the clear leading of God. Three are worthy of special attention:

The time is not right! Despite 16 years passing since the foundations of the temple had been laid, people were still arguing that the time for building had not come! They found time to build their own luxurious homes while neglecting the "house of God" (1:3-4).

Business is bad! The Jews had sown bountifully year after year but continued to reap a poor harvest. During this period, God had deprived the nation of His full blessing in an effort to chastise them for their neglect. "God punishes men in both ways," writes John Calvin, "both by withdrawing His blessing, so that the earth is parched, and the heaven gives no rain, and also, even when there is a good supply of the fruits of the earth, by preventing their satisfying, so that there is no real enjoyment of them. . . ." Men ought to be more sensitive to these providential directives of God in life. As Moore has written in his commentary *Haggai and Malachi* "the events of life are the hieroglyphics in which God records His feelings for us."

There isn't enough money to do the job! People complained that a paycheck went into pockets with holes (1:5-7)! No matter how much they brought in there was *never* enough to divert to outside needs and interests. Life was an endless treadmill going nowhere.

To these excuses God urges men "to consider their ways!" The nation was admonished not to dwell upon its misfortune but to busy itself with the work of God. Then God would bless. Such a commitment would involve the expenditure of funds and personal effort, but there was the accompanying promise of God's blessing (1:8) and presence (1:13).

The Second Message

The second message of Haggai (2:1-9) makes up a word of encouragement to those who would look at this new building and mourn when comparing it with the majestic and splendid edifice constructed during the reign of King Solomon. Confidence among the people was restored when Haggai declares that this new temple would be the recipient of far greater glory than that which had been bestowed upon the Solomonic structure.

The past is always irretrievable and no amount of effort could ever restore what God had taken in judgment. To the toilers who had become discouraged in the task, Haggai inspires to "be strong" and "take courage" (2:4-5). Now was not the time to sit down and deplore the lost glory of the past, but to stand in the strength of God's Spirit and fulfill the task at hand.

One is never guaranteed that the pursuit of godliness is void of struggle and frustration. True victory lies not so much in the freedom of trouble but in the joy of accomplishment. When final victory is wrought, no circumstance was too much. "Go on" is the message of Haggai's second sermon and the admonition to us all!

The Third Message

This third message of Haggai is praised by Everett Harrison in his *Introduction to the Old Testament* as ". . . the most concise statement to be found anywhere in the Old Testment of the tact that evil is far more penetrating and diffusive than goodness." This message deals with spiritual issues and draws its roots deep within the practices of ritual law in ancient Judaism.

Haggai points out that contact with holy flesh does not sanctify, but contact with that which was defiled did defile. Darby summarizes the point made clear by the prophet when writing, "That which is holy cannot sanctify unclean things; but an unclean thing defiles that which is holy, for holiness is exclusive with respect to evil."

Through these penetrating questions, Haggai taught the lesson that through neglect of the Lord and His temple, the people themselves, their offerings and all their works had become unclean in His sight.

The concluding part of this message is a promise to the nation that their obedience to the Lord in building the temple would bring a stop to the chastening so characteristic of the past 16 years. The blight and mildew responsible for the losses in agricultural productivity were God's punitive hand laid upon the nation; their obedience now would reap for them God's blessings on their labors!

The Fourth Message

The fourth and final message of Haggai (2:20-23) takes the form of a promise to Zerubbabel that, despite disturbances in the empires of the world, his safe keeping was guaranteed.

The reference to God "shaking the heavens and the earth" (2:21) is considered by Barnes to refer to "the convulsions of the Persian empire in the earliest years of Darius, when province after province sought to establish its own independence." Others, however, regard that significant expression to be too wide to be satisfied by any local fulfillment but reaching forth to a more distant accomplishment. Whatever the case, the prophet makes clear that no disturbance on heaven or earth could cause God to relent from fulfilling His promises to Israel. God has unconditionally and irrevocably committed Himself to Israel's ultimate blessing.

Conclusion

Few of the prophets could point to the success of their personal ministries. Some were told by God that their words would fall on deaf ears and others experienced personal suffering after they spoke (Heb. 11:36-37), but Haggai beheld a nation whose heart was pricked in conviction by the Spirit of God. The nation proceeded to build in accordance to God's desire and because of their work they were blessed. Obedience always leads to blessing!

11

Zechariah: God's
Message from the
Myrtle Grove

KEYS THAT UNLOCK ZECHARIAH

I. The Time of the Book: Zechariah was a Post-Exilic Prophet to the nation Judah.

II. The Contemporaries of the Prophet: Haggai and Ezra.

III. The Theme of the Book: God's plan is eternal.

IV. The Key Verses of the Book: "Rejoice greatly, O daughter of Zion! Shout in triumph, O daughter of Jerusalem! Behold, your king is coming to you. He is just and endowed with salvation, humble, and mounted on a donkey, even on a colt, the foal of a donkey. And I will cut off the chariot from Ephraim, and the horse from Jerusalem; and the bow of war will be cut off. And He will speak peace to the nations; and His dominion will be from sea to sea, and from the River to the ends of the earth" (Zech. 9:9-10).

V. Background Reading: Ezra 5:1—6:15

Zechariah was a contemporary of the prophet Haggai. The temple building had been neglected for 16 years until God raised up His spokesman, Haggai, to *arouse* the people to complete the task. Zechariah's message is supplemental to that of his contemporary as he seeks to *lead* a nation to a complete spiritual change. The extent of Zechariah's prophecies reach beyond the immediate situation and become universal in their scope. Freeman has commented, "The prophecy of Zechariah is to the Old Testament what the Book of the Revelation is to the New. It is the *Apocalypse* of the Old Testament which portrays God's future dealings with His chosen people."

Many of the clearest messianic teachings to be found in the Old Testament are included in Zechariah. Among the noteworthy are references to Christ as the Branch (3:8, 6:12); Christ as Shepherd (9:16, 11:11); Christ's entry into Jerusalem on a colt (9:9); the betrayal for 30 pieces of silver (11:12-13); the piercing of Christ's hands and feet (12:12); and His triumphal return to the Mount of Olives (14:3-8).

The prophecy falls into two major divisions: chapters 1 through 8 and 9 through 14. The first of these sections is primarily composed of eight visions of the prophet. Zechariah's final six chapters are verbal prophecies pertaining to that which is clearly future.

The purpose of Zechariah was best expressed by one commentator who writes, "The central purpose of the prophecies of Zechariah is to show that the glorification of Zion, the overthrow of Israel's enemies, and the universal reign of Messiah—in fact all the promises of Israel's future—would yet be realized in the distant future." This book that Luther referred to as "the quintessence of the prophets" looked beyond the present to the glory of the coming of Messiah.

The Message of the Visions

The eight visions of Zechariah are introduced by an initial plea by Jehovah for the nation to turn from the wickedness of the past (1:1-6). These verses plead with a restored nation not to repeat the willful folly of the past. Wordsworth writes, "no spiritual privileges will profit them without holiness, but will rather aggravate their guilt and increase their condemnation if they disobey God." This brief introduction is foundational to the fuller revelation to follow. Merrill F. Unger writes of these introductory verses in his *Commentary on Zechariah* that:

> . . . its theme strikes the keynote of the entire book and forms an indispensable introduction to it. The truth that it enunciates is one which runs throughout the revealed ways of God with man; namely, the appropriation and enjoyment of God's promises of blessing must be perfected by genuine repentance. . . . Although the immutability of God's Word and the continuity of His plans for Israel assure the fulfillment of these purposes, nevertheless the people are not to divorce divine grace from human responsibility.

Haggai's admonitions to the exiles had been responded to and the nation had again resumed the rebuilding of the temple. The visions of Zechariah were a timely answer to many of the perplexing questions that were being raised during this eventful period. While each vision had the immediate result of consolation and encouragement to the people of Zechariah's day, it is important to note, as Unger has observed, that they "bridge the centuries and extend to the period of the restoration of the kingdom of Israel. . . ." Complete fulfillment obviously lay in the future.

Three months after Zechariah's initial plea for repentance, the prophet was given eight visions. The fact that the prophet was capable of conversing freely with an angel, who acted as an interpreter of the visions, would argue for the fact that the prophet was alert and fully conscious. Apparently all eight visions recorded in this initial section of the book were delivered in the course of one night. The significant aspects of each message are included in the following review:

The Four Horsemen (1:7-17). As Judah's 70 years of predicted captivity (Jer. 25:11-12; 29:10) drew to a close, the nation must have known some perplexity as they attempted to comprehend the future program of God for them. The prophet is shown in this initial vision four horsemen who had patrolled the earth and had found things to be peaceful and quiet (1:11). This reference to tranquillity depicts life as it existed in the Middle East during the early years of Persian dominance.

In the midst of Israel's resettlement the Lord providentially reveals to the prophet Zechariah that He "is exceedingly jealous for Jerusalem and Zion" (1:14). Anger with the gentile nations is expressed (1:15) and a promise is given that the divine presence would once again return to Jerusalem (1:16) with its accompanying blessings (1:17).

This vision reinforced the prophetic urgings of Haggai while providing a source of encouragement and reassurance to a remnant that their history had been written in the annuls of heaven.

The Four Horns and Four Smiths (1:18-21). The second vision given to Zechariah anticipates the ultimate defeat of the nations who have oppressed Israel and a consequent removal of all obstacles to the nation's blessing.

The prophet is shown four horns that are identified as those forces which have been responsible for the scattering of the nations (1:19). The horn is frequently used in the Scripture as a symbol of power (Ps. 75:4-5, 92:10; Jer. 48:25; Dan. 7:24, 8:3-4; Amos 1:13; Rev. 17:12). It is clear from the angel's explanation that these horns represented great nations or empires who had oppressed, persecuted and forcibly deported Israel from their lands. The specific identity of the horns is debated, the prominent suggestions being either the nations Egypt, Assyria, Babylon and Medo-Persia or, with a more distant prophetic fulfillment in mind, Babylon, Medo-Persia, Greece and Rome (the same four powers portrayed to Daniel in Daniel, chapters 2 and 7).

Zechariah is then shown four "smiths" or craftsmen who are depicted as God's destroyers of the enemies of Israel and Judah. The prophet is reminded that the affairs of earth are superintended in heaven and that God's ultimate purpose will be accomplished!

The Immeasurable Greatness of Jerusalem (2:1-13). Zechariah's third vision is an amplification of that which has preceded. The prophet is shown a picture of Jerusalem's future prosperity and blessing. The first part of this vision (2:1-5) deals with the city and the conclusion of it (2:6-13) refers directly to the nation.

Zechariah was shown a man whose object was to measure the length and breadth of the city of Jerusalem. In the past the city was seen measured in preparation for judgment (see 2 Kings 23:13, Lam. 2:8), but now the act is seen as a dramatic representation of the fact that its future vastness would far exceed anything of the past. There would be no need for walls since Jehovah Himself promised to be their defense. He would be a protective wall of fire around the city. People would live in peace and freedom and would expand their borders at will.

The second part of the vision (2:6-13) makes reference to the nation's previous dispersions and guarantees their return from the far corners of the earth. Those that afflict Israel "touch the apple of God's eye" and are ripe for His judgment. In the future those who had spoiled Judah would themselves become a spoil. The tables were to be turned! Many other nations will join themselves to the Lord and will become His people.

While these promises were partially fulfilled during Zechariah's day, it seems apparent that their complete fulfillment awaits a future period.

The Cleansing of Joshua (3:1-10). In the three preceding visions Zechariah had been shown that the gentile nations would be judged for their treatment of Israel and that Israel would be ultimately blessed. Before restoration could take place, however, defilement must be removed.

In this vision the prophet sees Joshua, the new high priest, clothed in new garments and promised success in his endeavors if he remained faithful to Jehovah. The significance of Joshua's office is well expressed by Leupold in his *Exposi-*

tion of Zechariah who writes that the high priest

> represents and practically impersonates Israel in his holy office. For the nation he prays; for it he enters the holy place; he bears the nation's guilt. We must not, therefore, refer the issues and implications of this chapter to Joshua as an individual, nor merely to Joshua, the high priest. We must conclude that *his* condition is *Israel's* condition, *his* acquittal a typical way of expressing *theirs;* the words of comfort and assurance given him apply with equal validity to *them.*

This vision, then, concerns the cleansing of the priesthood as representative of the cleansing of the people.

A further prophecy concerning the coming of Messiah (the Branch) is given Zechariah in this vision. The analogy of the branch is not new to the prophetic writings (see Isa. 11:1, Job 14:7-9) and presents a picture, as Martin Luther wrote, "of the whole of theology and the works of God; that Christ did not come till the trunk had died and was altogether in a hopeless condition." Messiah's advent into the world would be in God's perfect time (Gal. 4:4).

The Seven Branched Lampstand (4:1-14). The fifth vision of the prophet was a word of encouragement to the leaders of Israel, Zerubbabel and Joshua. Zechariah was shown that human ability and effort were insufficient in themselves to accomplish God's purpose. God's work is only realized through His enablement!

In the vision, Zechariah saw a golden lampstand. The capability of the lamp was obviously dependent upon the energy source available to it. Without oil there could be no light. This lamp seen by Zechariah was attached to a seemingly inexhaustible energy source (4:3).

The prophet was quick to acknowledge his confusion with the symbols of that which he had seen. The angel explained that this was the word of Jehovah to the civil governor of Israel, Zerubbabel (4:6). He was to be reminded that no amount of personal might or power would be sufficient to accomplish the great task before the nation. Through God's enablement, however, the task would be accomplished. Zerubbabel was promised that the work to which he had been called would be accomplished in his lifetime (4:9). This encouragement to the nation's leader served as a reminder that the strength of his administration lay not just in his ability to rule but in the sufficiency of his God.

The angel later explains that the two olive trees symbolized the two anointed ones who stood by the Lord of the whole earth. Since only kings and priests were anointed it is generally agreed that the reference was to Zerubbabel and Joshua, the civil and religious leaders, who were God's mediators with His people.

The Flying Scroll (5:1-4). The sixth vision of the prophet is concerned with the cleansing and sanctification of the nation and the land. The stress is placed upon the holiness of God and the divine intolerance to sin.

Zechariah was shown a huge scroll, the size of which was about 30 feet by 15 feet. It was described by the accompanying angel as "the curse that is going forth over the whole land" (5:3). The scroll contained the names of those who had transgressed God's law and announced their certain judgment. No one could avoid the scroll's relentless pursuit. Frederick Tatford observes that "the nation and the land must be cleansed of every contamination, and the sinner must be dealt with in unmitigated justice. The minatory character of the vision was in startling and salutary contrast to the consolatory terms of the preceding visions. . . . God's holiness was at stake." Moore makes a similar observation about the implicit warning of the vision. He writes,

> There is something most vivid and appalling in this image of the hovering curse. It flies viewless and resistless, poising like a falcon over her prey, breathing a ruin the most dire and desolating, and when the blind and hardened offender opens his door to his ill-gotten gains, this mysterious roll, with its fire-tracery of wrath, enters into his habitation, and fastening upon his cherished idols, begins its dread work of retribution, and ceases not until the fabric of his guilty life has been totally and irredeemably consumed.

The message of this vision is significantly contemporary. God's standard of holiness has not been lowered and men today need the constant reminder of the Apostle John that those who claim to belong to Christ ought to behave as He did. Disregard for morality, laxity in general conduct and impurity of thought and word are completely irreconcilable with the unblemished purity of Christ. We dare not ignore God's message in this vision.

The Woman in the Ephah (5:5-11). The vision of the Flying Scroll was concerned with the sin of the individual; while this seventh vision focuses upon the cleansing of the nation from what one writer referred to as the "ungodly secularism and intense commercial preoccupation" that had gripped the nation.

Zechariah saw an ephah, a large container, which was identified as a representation of the sinful state of the people throughout Judah. The ephah was a commercial measure (see Exod. 16:36) and as such was a fitting symbol of trade and commernce. Merrill Unger, in his *Commentary on Zechariah,* indicates that commerical competitiveness was one of the observable products of Judah's 70 years in Babylon. While commerce is not wrong in itself, obsession for prosperity and greed for personal gain caused more than one to sacrifice their integrity. Laetsh points out that "the Lord demands a just ephah, full measure, integrity and honesty in selling and buying in all business and judicial transactions (Lev. 19:35 and following, Deut. 25:4-5, Ezek. 45:9 and following, and Micah 6:10-15)." Amos had earlier struck at the heart of the issue when writing that the people of Israel were "making the ephah small and the shekel great and falsifying the balances by deceit" (Amos 8:5).

The prophet observed a woman within the ephah, who the angel identified as the personification of wickedness. Apparently unwilling to accept the restriction of the ephah, she was endeavoring to secure liberty to roam at will. The angel, however, slammed the lid upon the mouth of the container. Two women (5:9) later come and lift the ephah between the earth and the heavens. Perplexed by what he had seen, Zechariah was told that the women were carrying it away to build an abode for it in Shinar.

The identify of the two women has been disputed. Some have concluded that they are representatives of God's justice; while others see them as depicting "apostate Christianity united in the last days to aspostate Judaism." Shinar and its implications are not as difficult. "Shinar," writes Smith, "is symbolic of wickedness and opposition to God. Shinar is the symbol of Satan's kingdom of wickedness." Kelly concurs and sees the imagery as "the idolatrous evil of the Jews derived from and sent back to Babylon." There an abode was built, far from Judah, to house and honor her.

These visions (the sixth and seventh) were intended to show the need for forsaking sin and the absolute necessity of removing from their midst the wicked standards that created a profitable environment for it!

The Four Chariots (6:1-8). The eight visions of Zechariah form something of a circle as now the prophet sees four chariots, who like the four horsemen of the first vision, exercise freedom and influence throughout the whole earth. "The first vision and the eighth," writes Barnes, "form together the framework in which the whole section (1:7−6:8) is set. The one appropriately begins, the other appropriately closes the series of visions. Neither is a theophany but each stands instead of a theophany. . . . In the first the angel of Jehovah appears and converses through the veil with Jehovah Himself. In the last the gate between heaven and earth is opened and the four spirits of heaven in the guise of chariots come forth."

The prophet saw four chariots pass between two mountains on their way to fulfill their appointed mission. The angel explained that the chariots represented the four spirits of the heavens which go forth into the earth from the immediate presence of God. Baron, in his book *The Servant of Jehovah*, suggests that these be understood as "either ideal appearances, personifying the forces and providential acts which God often uses in carrying out His judgments on the earth, or . . . angelic beings, or heavenly powers—those invisible messengers of His." Each chariot is drawn by a horse of a different color and is dispatched to one of the four corners of the earth.

Interpreters generally agree that that which is pictured here is the execution of judgment upon wickedness existing in the world. Previous visions spoke of the cleansing of Israel and now the prophet is shown the justice of God in action against the gentile nations throughout the world.

The visions of Zechariah provided encouragement to the remnant of Judah who had been restored to their land. God is seen in the visions as in complete control over the affairs of the earth. His eternal holiness is the standard unto which men should strive and all violators of this righteous standard will be judged. The nation had experienced the providential care and protection of God during their day and history will forever testify to God's continued faithfulness to His promises!

The remaining verses of the first section of Zechariah's prophecy deal with the symbolic crowning of Joshua (6:11-15) and with problems surrounding the matter of fasting (chapters 7 and 8).

The Message of the Future

The second and final section of the Book of Zechariah (chapters 9 through 14) constitute some of the most remarkable prophecies ever written. J. Sidlow Baxter has observed three main movements around which the Lord reveals to Zechariah facts concerning Israel's remarkable future. It will be around these three movements that our comments will be reserved:

Part I: The Coming Shepherd-King and Zion's Consequent Blessing (chapters 9 and 10). This movement begins with judgment being announced upon the nations surrounding Israel (9:1-8). The flow of the passage is interrupted at verse 9 with a parenthetic announcement of the coming of Israel's king, the Messiah. Israel is then promised eventual victory over her enemies (9:10-17). Chapter 10 announces additional blessings such as God removing wicked shepherds from their midst, Israel and Judah being reunited and God restoring the exiles to their land. Acceptance and submission to the coming Messiah precedes the blessing pronounced to the nation.

Part II: The Rejection of the Shepherd-King and the Tragic Results (chapter 11). The Messiah, Israel's true shepherd, was despised and rejected. The tragic consequences of their refusal to accept Christ's claims would result (and has resulted) in the nation being wasted by her present shepherds (11:4-14). A remarkable announcement concerning a coming false shepherd, who shall afflict and persecute Israel, concludes this chapter (11:15-17).

Part III. The Final Travail and Triumph of Zion: Jehovah's Victory (chapters 12, 13, and 14). Zechariah's prophecy comes to a climactic end with an announcement of Messiah's second coming (12:10—13:6) and the establishment of the millennial kingdom (14:1-21).

The travail of Israel will exist until the time of their ultimate victory. Jerusalem will be attacked by the nations, but God will grant deliverance. Gentile world power will be broken in that final day and Christ will rule in fulfillment of His promise.

The testimony of the prophets is that God is faithful. His promises are sure and true. May we never compromise God's Word and may He give us strength and boldness to proclaim it, without reservation, to a lost and floundering world!

12

Malachi: Prophet to the Indifferent

KEYS THAT UNLOCK MALACHI

I. The Time of the Book: Malachi is a Post-Exilic Prophet to Judah.

II. The Contemporaries of the Prophet: No other prophets minister during the period of Malachi's ministry.

III. The Theme of the Book: Appeal to Backsliders.

IV. The Key Verses of the Book: "Behold, I am going to send my messenger, and he will clear the way before Me. And the Lord, whom you seek, will suddenly come to His temple; and the messenger of covenant, in whom you delight, behold, he is coming, say the Lord of hosts. But who can endure the day of His coming? And who can stand when He appears? For He is like a refiner's fire and like fullers' soap. From the days of your fathers you have turned aside from My statutes, and have not kept them. Return to Me, and I will return to you," says the Lord of hosts. "But you say, 'How shall we return?' " (3:1-2, 7)

V. Background Reading: Nehemiah 13:1-31

The prophecy of Malachi concludes the revelation from God for a period of no less than 400 years. As Nagelsbach has written, "Malachi is like a late evening, which brings a day to a close; but he is also like the morning dawn, which bears a glorious day in its womb."

Malachi was a critic of the conditions of his day. The prophet was characterized by Henry McKeating as ". . . first and foremost a man of God. He is a religious visionary. His criticisms, therefore, were felt to have a force and authority with which we should not credit the criticism of any modern functionary." Keil recognizes the primary burden of the prophet to be his concern over the spiritual inconsistency of the restored remnant. He writes that the book

> . . . contains one single prophecy, the character of which is condemnatory throughout. Starting with the love which the Lord has shown to His people (1:2-5), the prophet proves that not only do the priests profane the name of the Lord by an unholy performance of the service at the altar (1:6, 2:9), but the people also repudiate their divine calling both by heathen marriages and frivolous divorces (2:10-16), and by their murmuring at the delay of the judgment; whereas the Lord will soon reveal Himself as a just judge, and before His coming will send His messenger, the prophet Elijah, to warn the ungodly and lead them to repentance, and then suddenly come to His temple as the expected angel of the covenant, to refine the sons of Levi, punish the sinners who have broken the covenant, and by exterminating the wicked, as well as by blessing the godly with salvation and righteousness, make the children of Israel the people of His possession (3:17—4:6).

Internal evidence argues that Malachi probably ministered around 425 B.C. The temple, rebuilt during the days of Haggai and Zechariah, was completed (1:10) by the time of this prophecy and there had been a deterioration in the conduct of the priesthood and a disregard for the payment of tithes on the part of the people (1:12-14; 3:8-10) which implies a lapse of some years after the construction of the building. Divorce was prevalent and many in the nation had married foreign women (2:14-26). Although Nehemiah had to deal with conditions that were similar, they seemingly were not as widespread (Neh., chapter 13). At the time of Malachi's writing, a Persian governor was ruling in the land (1:8) who, by implication, accepted gifts and tribute. Nehemiah never did so during his governorship (Neh. 5:14-15) which would argue that he was not serving in the capacity at the time of this writing. In the light of this evidence our ascribed date seems justified.

Features of the Book

The major purpose of the Book of Malachi is to appeal to Israel to repent of her sin and return to the Lord. This appeal is given in view of God's love, the present sin and the coming day of judgment for the guilty and blessing for the godly.

The primary thoughts of the book are expressed in its two key verses: "Behold, He shall come, saith Jehovah of Hosts; but who may abide the day of His coming" (see 3:1-2); and "Return unto me, and I will return unto you, saith Jehovah of hosts" (see 3:7).

The most unusual feature of the book is its unique style. Frederick Tatford writes that "the book is composed of a series of paragraphs cast in dialectical form. First a charge was made against the people, who at once provocatively questioned the accuracy, significance or justification of the charge, which the prophet then defended logically with detailed evidence and argument, driving home the charge with renewed force. There is nothing comparable in the pages of the Old Testament." Ewald refers to this as "the dialogistic method," and I make reference to his style in my *Analytical Survey of the Bible* as the "didactic-dialectic" method.

It should be noted that more than half of the book deals with the deplorable conditions characteristic of the day; while the predictive element is restricted to the final two chapters.

The Outline of the Book

The Book of Malachi can be divided into six sections easily

distinguishable within the text. The sections, or "oracles" as they are referred to (1:1) are as follows: 1:2-5; 1:6—2:9; 2:10-16; 2:17—3:5; 3:6-12; 3:13—4:3. A superscription (1:1) precedes the narrative and a brief conclusion (4:4-6) warns the nation to be obedient to the Law of Moses and promises that a forerunner, after the figure of Elijah, would announce to the world the future Day of the Lord.

The First Oracle

The first oracle of Malachi (1:2-5) reaffirms God's great love for the nation Israel. This love had been demonstrated in the divine selection of Jacob over his older brother Esau. God had made it perfectly clear throughout the Old Testament that this love was not based upon the merits of Jacob's descendants. The nation was specifically informed by Moses that, "The Lord did not set His love on you nor choose you because you were more in number than any of the peoples, for you were the fewest of all peoples, but because the Lord loved you and kept the oath which He had sworn to your forefathers, the Lord brought you out by a mighty hand, and redeemed you from the house of slavery, from the hand of Pharoah, king of Egypt" (Deut. 7:7-8). God's love was bestowed upon Israel by a sovereign God for no reason comprehensible to man.

The nation responded to the statement of unreserved love by mockingly questioning, ". . . How hast Thou loved us? . . ." (1:2). The prophet utilizes the literary effect unique to his writing to emphasize the astonishing disregard for Jehovah so much in evidence at his time. Their interrogation reflected the unpardonable contempt they showed toward God. "This ingratitude," writes Laetsch, "was rooted in their selfishness, the prevailing sin of post-exilic Judaism, which finally led to their own rejection of the Lord." The prevailing prosperity of the time had destroyed spirituality and, in the words of Frederick Tatford, "had fostered a self-centered attitude which was really as objectionable as the idolatry of pre-exilic days."

Despite their attitude, God's covenant obligations to the nation would be graciously fulfilled. Harrison writes "that Edom was devastated for her wickedness while by contrast Israel would soon learn that God would be magnified in her. Whereas Edom would never recover her ancestral home, the elect nation would inhabit Mount Zion in glory." Such irrefutable proof of God's supreme interest and care for Israel is eloquent testimony that their exalted future is guaranteed!

The Second Oracle

Malachi's second message (1:6–2:9) denounced the priestly class for its failure to supply moral and spiritual leadership to the nation.

The literary technique characteristic to Malachi again lends forcefulness to his appeal. To every accusation made by the prophet, a challenge was raised demonstrating the deep-rooted indifference by the priests to God's commands. Such deplorable attitudes were reprehensible because of the effect upon the people and would be decisively responded to by God in judgment. William Kelly in his *Lectures on the Minor Prophets* deals with the crux of the issue when observing:

> The higher the relation, the greater the danger where God is not before the soul. It is not only that sin in such is more serious, but also there is greater exposure to it. A priest has to walk not merely as becomes a man outside the sanctuary, but as one who goes into it. There was a more complete consecration in the case of a priest than with an Israelite; and familiarity with the presence of God, unless it be kept up in His fear, borders on contempt."

The three specific charges against the priesthood deserve our special consideration.

Their sacrifices were improper (1:8-14). The Law of Moses required that offerings presented to God be unblemished (Lev. 4:3, 9:2). The tragedy of Malachi's day was that blind, lame and sick animals were being offered in direct violation of the clear prohibitions of the law. The priests apparently condoned and probably encouraged this activity. Maclaren takes the view that the priests "were probably dishonest as well as mean, because the worshipers would bring sound beasts, and the priests, for their own profit, slipped in a worthless animal, and kept the valuable one for themselves. They had become so habituated to this piece of economic religion, that they saw no harm in it." G. Campbell Morgan concurs when he summarizes the situation in his *Studies in Malachi* writing, "these men have lost the sense of what worship means in that they have retained the finest of the flock for themselves, and brought to the altar that which engenders its contempt, simply to keep up the form of sacrifice and the appearance which they so much covet." Malachi points out that they would never think of offering unacceptable gifts to their civil governor (1:8) and yet they repeatedly offered to God their leftovers. Tatford finds a parallel in the attitudes of many today when he writes, "We offer God what we do not want for ourselves. The time, talent and ability, which should be devoted to His service, are employed for our own ends, and we condescendingly give Him what is left over."

Their instruction was corrupted (2:6-8). A second charge levelled against the priesthood of Israel by Malachi concerned their corrupt teaching. The divine standard in that regard is expressed by the prophet in Malachi 2:7: "For the lips of a priest should preserve knowledge and man should seek instruction from his mouth." The priesthood had miserably failed in their commissioned responsibilities and this contemptible behavior and disregard for their work made them ripe for punishment.

Their example was abominable (2:8). The results of their insensitivity were vividly apparent in the lives of those to whom they ministered. Malachi charges, "you have caused many to stumble . . ." (2:8). The commitment of the congregation reflected the commitment of their leader! Those who looked for leadership and direction stumbled when observing the compromise and low regard the priests placed on things pertaining to the law. Example is a powerful teacher and frequently speaks a louder word than that which is verbally uttered. The group which had the greatest opportunity to influence life in Israel had miserably failed!

The prophet declares a fourfold judgment upon the unrepentant priests. His message was that their blessings would be curses (2:2), their offspring rebuked (2:3), their offerings rejected (2:3) and their influence despised (2:9). God had made a special covenant with Levi and his descendants and this punitive action was evidence that He would abide by its provisions (2:4-5).

The Third Oracle

The third message of the prophet (2:10-16) dealt with the question of mixed marriages and divorce. Jews in Malachi's day were divorcing their Jewish wives in order that they might marry foreign women. These actions were abhorrent to God who clearly affirms that the resultant sufferings were the sole responsibility of the participants.

The sickness bears evidence of the disease! Hengstenberg comments, "He who annuls the distinction between an Israelite and a heathen woman proves by that very action that he has already annihilated the distinction between the God of Israel and the idols of the heaven, that he has no longer the theocratic consciousness of God." This lack of "God-consciousness" had led to more than one personal disaster. God affirms His view on divorce in Malachi 2:16, "For I hate divorce . . ." and pleads for the nation to stop this treacherous behavior.

The Fourth Oracle

God had become so displeased with the rationalization of the people for their sinful behavior and their complaints that there is no justice in life that He would shortly manifest Himself in judgment. Malachi's fourth message (2:17—3:5) prophesies this coming of God in judgment which would serve as a refining measure resulting again in God's blessing upon the offerings of His people (3:4).

The Fifth Oracle

The fifth message of the prophet (3:6-12) establishes a clear link between the current social and economic distress to an attitude of indifference by the people toward the payment of tithes.

The legal requirements of the nation are summarized well by T. V. Moore in his commentary entitled *Haggai and Malachi*. He writes

> "The tithes required by the Mosaic law were, first, a tenth of all that remained after the first-fruits (which belonged to God and must be given to Him), which tenth was God's as the original proprieter of the soil, and was paid to the Levites for their maintenance (Lev. 27:30-32). Secondly, from this tenth the Levites paid a tenth to the priests (Num. 18:26-28). Thirdly, a second tenth was paid by the people for the entertainment of the Levites and their own families at the tabernacle (Deut. 12:18). Fourthly, another tithe was paid every third year for the poor, widows, orphans, etc. (Deut. 14:28-29).

The prophet declares that the withholding of tithes was not only a robbery of God, but a defrauding of priests, the widows, fatherless and strangers. God's curse had befallen the nation because of this neglect. Writes Packard:

> ... they withheld tithes notwithstanding that God had already visited them with severe punishment, which aggravated their guilt. They had been cursed ... with failure of the harvest and famine. Their curse corresponded to their sin. As they had refused to give God His due by offering defective sacrifices and by withholding the tithes and offerings, so had He withheld from them the products of the field.

The way to blessing is always associated with obedience! If the nation would obey God by bringing Him tithes, He would reciprocate by opening for them the windows of heaven. This phrase, "the windows of heaven," comments Tatford,

> ... is used only four times in the Old Testament. The earlier occurrences were first in Genesis 7:11, where it is said that the windows of heaven were opened to allow the outpouring of the heavy rains which contributed to the judgment of the flood of

Noah's day. The second and third were in 2 Kings 7:2, 19, where they were employed in disbelief of the divine prediction made through the mouth of Elisha. Malachi's prophecy the floodgates were to be opened, not in judgment, but in richest blessing.

The paradox is clear: sacrificial giving reaps dividends from God!

The Sixth Oracle

Why do the righteous suffer and the ungodly prosper? This question so frequently raised provided the impetus for Malachi's final message (3:13—4:3).

There were those who argued that "it is vain to serve God" (3:14). They spoke of their religious activity, vainly alluding to their fasting and mourning. Earnestly they pursued the form of religion only to receive the rebuke of God. Until their hearts are purified, however, their activity is but sham piety.

In the midst of that which is counterfeit, God always has a remnant of faithful ones and it is their godly walk that will reap for them eternal blessing. The promise of that reward (3:16-17) precedes the description of the wrath of God (4:1-3) that will destroy the wicked. This final Old Testament description of the Day of the Lord is viewed by George Adam Smith to be unparalleled in Scripture. He writes:

> The apocalypse of this last judgment is one of the grandest in all Scripture. To the wicked it shall be a terrible fire, root and branch shall be burned out, but to the righteous a fair morning of God, as when dawn comes to those who have been sick and sleepless through the black night, and its beams bring healing, even as to the popular belief of Israel it was the rays of the morning sun which distilled the dew. They break into life and energy, like young calves leaping from the dark pen into the early sunshine. To this morning landscape a grim figure is added. They shall tread down the wicked and the arrogant like ashes beneath their feet.

This day, previously described in Joel 1:15; 2:1-2, 31; 3:16; Zephaniah 1:15-18; Amos 5:18, and so forth, marks the final time when God will intervene in the affairs of men.

Conclusion

The final three verses of Malachi exhort the people to repentance and to a renewed observance of the law. The prophet announces the coming of Elijah (probably as Keil and others suggest, a referral to John the Baptist who came "in the spirit of Elijah") who, like others before him, would warn men and awaken men to repentance. It is only through repentance that God can restore that which has been lost to sin and apart from it (repentance) only His wrath remains (4:6)!

ADDITIONAL STUDY GUIDES IN THIS SERIES . . .

GENESIS, John P. Burke.

EXODUS, Tom Julien.

DEUTERONOMY, Bernard N. Schneider.

JOSHUA, JUDGES & RUTH, John J. Davis.

1 & 2 SAMUEL & 1 KINGS 1-11, John J. Davis.

KINGS & CHRONICLES, John C. Whitcomb.

PROVERBS, Charles W. Turner.

DANIEL, Robert D. Culver.

MAJOR THEMES FROM THE MINOR PROPHETS, Gerald H. Twombly.

MATTHEW, Harold H. Etling.

GOSPEL OF JOHN, Homer A. Kent, Jr.

ACTS, Homer A. Kent, Jr.

ROMANS, Herman A. Hoyt.

1 CORINTHIANS, James L. Boyer.

GALATIANS, Homer A. Kent, Jr.

EPHESIANS, Tom Julien.

PHILIPPIANS, David L. Hocking.

COLOSSIANS AND PHILEMON, Homer A. Kent, Jr.

1 & 2 TIMOTHY, Dean Fetterhoff.

HEBREWS, Herman A. Hoyt.

JAMES, Roy R. Roberts.

1, 2, 3 JOHN, Raymond E. Gingrich.

REVELATION, Herman A. Hoyt.

THE WORLD OF UNSEEN SPIRITS, Bernard N. Schneider.

THE HOLY SPIRIT AND YOU, Bernard N. Schneider.

PROPHECY, THINGS TO COME, James L. Boyer.

PULPIT WORDS TRANSLATED FOR PEW PEOPLE, Charles W. Turner.

SWEETER THAN HONEY, Jesse B. Deloe *(A guide to effective Bible study and the background of how we got our Bible).*

THE FAMILY FIRST, Kenneth O. Gangel.

LESSONS IN LEADERSHIP FROM THE BIBLE, Kenneth O. Gangel.

Obtain from your local Christian bookstore or by mail from BMH Books, P.O. Box 544, Winona Lake, Ind. 46590.